*Ah, Wil...*

## A COMEDY OF RECOLLECTION
## IN THREE ACTS

### *By* EUGENE O'NEILL

## SAMUEL FRENCH, INC.

| | |
|---|---|
| 45 West 25th Street | NEW YORK 10010 |
| 7623 Sunset Boulevard | HOLLYWOOD 90046 |
| *LONDON* | *TORONTO* |

Copy of program of the first performance of "AH, WIL-
DERNESS," as produced at The Guild Theatre, New York:

THE THEATRE GUILD, Inc.

Presents

## AH, WILDERNESS!

*A New Play*

*By* EUGENE O'NEILL

*With*

GEORGE M. COHAN

The Production Directed by Philip Moeller
Settings Designed by Robert Edmond Jones

### CAST

NAT MILLER, *owner of the "Evening Globe"*
—*George M. Cohan*
ESSIE, *his wife*.................*Marjorie Marquis*
ARTHUR, *their son*..............*William Post, Jr.*
RICHARD, *their son* .............*Elisha Cook, Jr.*
MILDRED, *their daughter*...........*Adelaide Bean*
TOMMY, *their son*...........*Walter Vonnegut, Jr.*
SID DAVIS, *Essie's brother, reporter on the "Wat-
erbury Standard"* ............. *Gene Lockhart*
LILY MILLER, *Nat's sister* ....... *Eda Heinemann*
DAVID McCOMBER, *dry-goods merchant*
—*Richard Sterling*
MURIEL McCOMBER, *his daughter*....*Ruth Gilbert*
WINT SELBY, *a classmate of Arthur's at Yale*
—*John Wynne*
BELLE ...........................*Ruth Holden*
NORA ...................... *Ruth Chorpenning*
BARTENDER ................. *Donald McClelland*
SALESMAN ........................ *John Butler*

3

ORIGINAL PROGRAM—*Continued*

SYNOPSIS OF SCENES

## ACT I

SCENE I—*Sitting-room of the Miller home in a large small-town in Connecticut. Early morning, July 4, 1906.*
SCENE II. *Dining-room of the Miller home. Evening of the same day.*

## ACT II

SCENE I. *Back room of a bar in a small hotel. 10 o'clock the same night.*
SCENE II. *The Miller sitting-room. A little after 10 o'clock the same night.*

## ACT III

SCENE I. *The Miller sitting-room. About 1 o'clock the following afternoon.*
SCENE II. *A strip of beach on the harbor. About 9 o'clock that night.*
SCENE III. *The Miller sitting-room. About 10 o'clock the same night.*

## DESCRIPTION OF CHARACTERS

TOMMY. *A chubby, sun-burnt boy of eleven, with dark eyes, blond hair wetted and plastered down in a part and a shiny, good-natured face.*

MILDRED *is fifteen, tall and slender, with big, irregular features, resembling her father to the complete effacing of any pretense at prettiness. But her big, gray eyes are beautiful; she has vivacity and a fetching smile, and everyone thinks of her as an attractive girl.*

ARTHUR. *He is the eldest of the Miller children who are still living home; is nineteen. He is tall, heavy, barrel-chested and muscular, the type of football linesman of that period, with a square, stolid face, small blue eyes and thick sandy hair. His manner is solemnly collegiate.*

MRS. MILLER *is around fifty, a short, stout woman, with fading light brown hair sprinkled with gray, who must have been decidedly pretty as a girl in a round-faced, cute, small-featured, wide-eyed fashion. She has big brown eyes, soft and maternal—a bustling, mother-of-a-family manner.*

LILY MILLER, *her sister-in-law, is forty-two, tall, dark, thin. She conforms outwardly to the conventional type of old-maid school teacher, even to wearing glasses. But behind the glasses her gray eyes are gentle and tired, and her whole atmosphere is one of shy kindliness. Her voice*

5

*presents the greatest contrast to her appearance
—soft and full of sweetness.*

**NAT MILLER** *is in his late fifties, a tall, dark, spare
man, a little stoop-shouldered, more than a little
bald. NAT'S long face has large, irregular, undistinguished features, but he has fine, shrewd,
humorous gray eyes.*

**SID DAVIS**, *his brother-in-law, is forty-five, short and
fat, bald-headed, with the Puckish face of a
Peck's Bad Boy who has never grown up.*

**RICHARD** *is sixteen, just out of high school. In appearance he is a perfect blend of father and
mother, so much so that each is convinced he is
the image of the other. He has his mother's
light-brown hair, his father's gray eyes; his features are neither large nor small; he is of
medium height, neither fat nor thin. One would
not call him a handsome boy; neither is he
homely. But he is definitely different from both
of his parents, too. There is something of extreme sensitiveness added—a restless, apprehensive, defiant, shy, dreamy, self-conscious intelligence about him. In manner he is alternately
plain, simple boy and a posey actor solemnly
playing a role.*

**DAVID McCOMBER** *is a thin, dried-up little man with
a head too large for his body perched on a
scrawny neck, and a long solemn horse face with
deep-set little black eyes, a blunt formless nose
and a tiny slit of a mouth. He is about the same
age as Miller but is entirely bald, and looks ten
years older.*

**NORA** *is a clumsy, heavy-handed, heavy-footed, long-
jawed, beamingly good-natured young Irish girl
—a "greenhorn."*

WINT *is nineteen, a classmate of Arthur's at Yale. He is a typical, good-looking college boy of the period, not the athletic but the hell-raising sport type. He is tall, blond, dressed in extreme collegiate cut.*

BELLE *is twenty, a rather pretty peroxide blonde, a typical college "tart" of the period, and of the cheaper variety, dressed with tawdry flashiness. But she is a fairly recent recruit to the ranks, and is still a bit remorseful behind her make-up and defiantly careless manner.*

BARTENDER. *A stocky young Irishman with a foxily cunning, stupid face and a cynically wise grin.*

SALESMAN. *He is a stout, jowly-faced man in his late thirties, dressed with cheap nattiness, with the professional breeziness and jocular, kid-'em-along manner of his kind.*

MURIEL McCOMBER *is fifteen, going on sixteen. She is a pretty girl with a plump, graceful little figure, fluffy, light-brown hair, big naive wondering dark eyes, a round dimpled face, a soft melting drawly voice.*

# AH, WILDERNESS!

## ACT ONE

### Scene I

*Sitting-room of the Miller home in a large small-
town in Connecticut—about seven-thirty in the
morning of July 4th, 1906.*

*The room is fairly large, homely looking and
cheerful in the morning sunlight, furnished with
scrupulous medium-priced tastelessness of the
period. Beneath the two windows, Right, a sofa
with silk and satin cushions stands against the
wall. Above sofa, a bookcase with glass doors,
filled with cheap sets, extends along the remain-
ing length of wall. In the rear wall, Right Center,
is a double doorway with sliding doors and portieres, leading into a dark, windowless back
parlor. At Left of this doorway another bookcase, this time a small, open one, crammed with
boys' and girls' books and the best-selling novels
of many past years—books the family really
have read. To the Left Center is the mate of
the double doorway at Right Center, with sliding
doors and portieres, this one leading to a well-
lighted front parlor. In the upper Left wall, a
screen door opens on a porch. Farther forward
in this wall are two windows, with a writing*

9

*desk and a chair above them. At Right Center
is a big, round table with a green shaded reading
lamp, the cord of the lamp running up to one
of five sockets in the chandelier above. Four
chairs are grouped around the table—two rock-
ers at Left, Right, rear of it; two armchairs
Right and Left in front. A medium-priced,
inoffensive rug covers most of the floor. At Left
Center an armchair; down Left a rocker. The
walls are papered white with a cheerful ugly
blue design. Chairs grouped about table Right
are numbered from one to four to simplify direction.*

    *Armchair below and* R. *of table is chair #1.
Rocking chair above and* R. *of table is chair #2.
Rocking chair above and* L. *of table is chair #3,
and armchair below and* L. *of table is #4.*

VOICES *are heard in a conversational tone from the
dining-room beyond the back parlor, where the
family are just finishing breakfast. Then* MRS.
MILLER'S *voice, raised commandingly: "Tommy!
Come back here and finish your milk!" At the
same moment,* TOMMY *appears in the doorway
from the back parlor—a chubby, sun-burnt boy
of eleven with dark eyes, blond hair wetted and
plastered down in a part, and a shiny, good-
natured face, a rim of milk visible about his lips.
Bursting with bottled-up energy on the Fourth,
he nevertheless has hesitated obediently at his
mother's call.          (WARN Crackers.)*

TOMMY. *(Calls back pleadingly as he wipes milk
from his upper lip)* Aw, I'm full, Ma. And I said
"excuse me" and you said "all right." *(Reaches door
up* L. *His father's voice is heard speaking to his
mother.* MILLER—*"Oh, let him run about." Then she*

*calls: "All right, Tommy!" And* TOMMY *asks eager-ly in doorway up* L.) Can I go out now?

MOTHER'S VOICE. *(Correctingly)* May I!

TOMMY. *(Fidgetting, but obediently)* May I, Ma?

MOTHER'S VOICE. Yes. (TOMMY *jumps for the screen door to the porch like a sprinter released by the starting shot.)*

FATHER'S VOICE. *(Shouts after him from off stage* R.C.) But you set off your crackers away from the house, remember! *(But* TOMMY *is already through the screen door, which he leaves open behind him.)*

*(A moment later the family appear* R.C. *from the back parlor, coming from the dining-room. First is* MILDRED. MILDRED *is fifteen, tall and slender, with big, irregular features, resembling her father to the complete effacing of any pretence at prettiness. But her big, gray eyes are beautiful. She has vivacity and a fetching smile, and every-one thinks of her as an attractive girl. She is dressed in shirtwaist and skirt in the fashion of the period. She runs to the screen door up* L., *looks out and laughs as she calls.)*

MILDRED. Look out for your hand, Tommy!

*(*ARTHUR *enters as* MILDRED *calls to* TOMMY. *He crosses to upper* R. *end of table* R. *and begins to fill his pipe. He is the eldest of the Miller chil-dren who are still living home; is nineteen. He is tall, heavy, barrel-chested and muscular, the type of football linesman of that period, with a square, stolid face, small blue eyes and thick, sandy hair. His manner is solemnly collegiate. He is dressed in the latest college fashion of that day, which has receded a bit from the extreme of preceding years, but still runs to padded*

*shoulders and pants half pegged at the top and so small at their wide-cuffed bottoms that they cannot be taken off with shoes on.) (CRACK-ERS—3 small.)*

MILDRED. *(Inquisitively, as* ARTHUR *appears)* Where are you going today, Art? *(Crosses to* L. *of* ARTHUR.)

ARTHUR. *(With superior dignity below chair #2)* That's my business. *(He ostentatiously takes from his pocket a tobacco pouch with a big Y and class numerals stamped on it, and a heavy bulldog briar pipe with silver Y and numerals, 08, and starts filling the pipe.)*

MILDRED. *(Teasingly)* Bet I know, just the same! Want me to tell you her initials? E. R.! *(She laughs and crosses to sofa down* R. ARHTUR *is pleased by this insinuation at his lady-killing activities, yet finds it beneath his dignity to reply. He lights his pipe and picks up the local morning paper and slouches back into the armchair #2, beginning to whistle "Oh, Waltz Me Around Again, Willie," as he scans the headlines.* MILDRED *sits on the sofa at* R., *front. Meanwhile their mother and their* AUNT LILY, *their father's sister, have appeared, following them from* R.C. *parlor.* MRS. MILLER *is around fifty, a short, stout woman with fading light brown hair sprinkled with gray, who must have been decidedly pretty as a girl in a round-faced, cute, small-featured, wide-eyed fashion. She has big, brown eyes, soft and maternal—a bustling, mother-of-a-family manner. She is dressed in shirtwaist and skirt.* LILY MILLER, *her sister-in-law, is forty-two, tall, dark, thin. She conforms outwardly to the conventional type of old-maid school teacher, even to wearing glasses. But behind the glasses her gray eyes are gentle and tired, and her whole atmosphere is one of shy kindliness.*

*Her voice presents the greatest contrast to her appearance—soft and full of sweetness. She, also, is dressed in a shirt-waist and skirt.)*

MRS. MILLER. *(As they appear)* Getting milk down him is like— *(Suddenly she is aware of the screen door standing half open. Crossing to screen door up* L.) Goodness, look at that door he's left open! The house will be alive with flies! I've told him again—and again—and that's all the good it does! It's just a waste of breath! *(She slams the door shut, then crosses to table* R. *and gets a magazine, then crosses to rocking chair down* L. *and fans herself with magazine as she talks.)*

LILY. *(Smiling)* Well, you can't expect a boy to remember to shut doors—on the Fourth of July. *(She goes diffidently to the straight-backed chair before the desk at* L., *leaving the comfortable chairs to the* OTHERS. *Gets towel from desk and starts to sew.)*

MRS. MILLER. That's you all over—Lily—always making excuses for him. You'll have him spoiled to death in spite of me. Phew, I'm hot, aren't you? This is going to be a scorcher. *(She begins to rock, fanning herself. Ad libs. to* LILY, *paying no attention to* MILLER *and* SID. *Meanwhile, her husband and her brother have appeared from* R.C. *parlor, both smoking cigars.* NAT MILLER *is in his late fifties, a tall, dark, spare man, a little stoop-shouldered, more than a little bald, dressed with an awkward attempt at sober respectability imposed upon an innate heedlessness of clothes.* ARTHUR *faces up and looks at* MILLER *and* SID *when they enter.* MILLER's *long face has large, irregular, undistinguished features, but he has fine, shrewd, humorous gray eyes.* SID DAVIS, *his brother-in-law, is forty-five, short and fat, bald-headed, with the Puckish face of a Peck's Bad Boy who has never grown up. He is dressed in what had*

*once been a very natty loud light suit but is now a*
*shapeless and faded nondescript in cut and color.)*
             *(WARN Crackers—12 small, 1 loud.)*

SID. *(Overlap cues as they appear. Comes in first and crosses to up* C.) Oh, I like the job first rate, Nat. Waterbury's a nifty old town with the lid off, when you get to know the ropes. I rang in a joke in one of my stories that tickled the folks there pink. *(Faces* MILLER) Waterwagon—Waterbury—Waterloo!

MILLER. *(Grinning, crosses to chair #3)* Darn good!

SID. *(Pleased)* I thought it was pretty fair myself. (MILLER *sits chair #3. Goes on a bit ruefully, as if oppressed by a secret sorrow)* Yes, you can see life in Waterbury, all right—that is, if you're looking for life in Waterbury!

MRS. MILLER. *(Looks at* SID, *thinking he has said something humorous)* What's that about Waterbury, Sid?

SID. I was saying it's all right in its way—but there's no place like home. *(As if to punctuate this remark, there begins a series of BANGS from just beyond the porch outside, as* TOMMY *inaugurates his celebration by setting off a package of firecrackers. The assembled family jump in their chairs.* SID *chuckles.)*       *(CRACKERS—12 small, 1 loud.)*

MRS. MILLER. That boy! *(She rushes to the screen door up* L. *and out on the porch, calling.* MILDRED *rises; crosses to screen door.* SID *follows her to up* L.; *looks out after her.)* Tommy! You mind what your Pa told you! You take your crackers out in the back yard, you hear me!

TOMMY. *(Off stage)* All right, Ma.

ARTHUR. *(Frowning scornfully)* Fresh kid! He did it on purpose to scare us.

MILLER. *(Grinning through his annoyance)* Darned youngster! He'll have the house afire before the day's out.

SID. *(Grins and sings; crosses to* C.)
"Dunno what ter call 'im
But he's mighty like a Rose-velt."
*(They* ALL *laugh.)*

LILY. Sid, you crazy! (SID *beams at her.* MRS. MILLER *comes back from the porch, still fuming; leaves door open.* MILDRED *closes door; stands looking out after* TOMMY, *laughing.)*

MRS. MILLER. *(Crosses to rocker down* L.) Well, I've made him go out back at last. Now we'll have a little peace. *(Sits in rocker. CRACKERS—6 small. As if to contradict this, the BANG of firecrackers and torpedoes begins from the rear of the house,* L., *and continues at intervals throughout the scene, not nearly so loud as the first explosion, but sufficiently emphatic to form a disturbing punctuation to the conversation.* MILDRED *exits up* L.; *closes screen door after her.)*

MILLER. Well, what's on the tappee for all of you today? Sid, you're coming to the Sachem Club picnic with me, of course.

SID. *(A bit embarrassedly)* You bet!—That is, if—

MRS. MILLER. *(Regarding her brother with smiling suspicion)* Hmmm! I know what that Sachem Club picnic's always meant!

LILY. *(Breaks in, in a forced joking tone that conceals a deep earnestness)* No, not this time, Essie. Sid's a reformed character since he's been on the paper in Waterbury. *(Slight reaction from* SID.) At least, that's what he swore to me last night.

SID. *(Avoiding her eyes, humiliated—joking it off)* Pure as the driven snow, that's me. They're running me for president of the W.C.T.U. *(They* ALL *laugh.* ARTHUR *laughs longest.)*

MRS. MILLER. *(Rises, laughing)* Sid, you're a caution. *(Crosses and puts magazine down on table,* R.C.)

You turn everything into a joke. But you be careful, you hear?

LILY. Oh, I know he'll be careful today. Won't you, Sid?

SID. *(Crosses to* LILY, *more embarrassed than ever —joking it off melodramatically)* Lily, I swear to you if any man offers me a drink, I'll kiil him—that is, if he changes his mind! *(They* ALL *laugh except* LILY, *who bites her lip and stiffens.)*

MRS. MILLER. No use talking to him, Lily. We can only hope for the best.

MILLER. *(Overlap)* Now, you women stop picking on Sid. (MILDRED *enters up* L. *and crosses via upstage to up* R.) It's the Fourth of July and even a downtrodden newspaper man has a right to enjoy himself when he's on his holiday. (SID *nods "Yes")*

MRS. MILLER. I wasn't thinking only of Sid.

SID. *(After a furtive glance at the stiff and silent* LILY—*changes the subject abruptly by turning to* ARTHUR. *Crosses to* C.) How are you spending the festive Fourth, Boola-Boola? (ARTHUR *stiffens dignifiedly.)*

MILDRED. *(Teasingly, quickly, crossing to above* ARTHUR) I can tell you, if he won't. *(Crosses to sofa, down* R.)

MRS. MILLER. *(Smiling, crosses to* L.) Off to the Rands', I suppose.

ARTHUR. *(With dignity)* I and Bert Turner are taking Elsie and Ethel Rand canoeing. And this evening I'm staying at the Rands' for dinner. (SID *crosses to door up* L.)

MILLER. What about you, Mid?

MILDRED. *(Crosses to and looking out window, down* R.) I'm going to the beach to Anne Culver's.

MILLER. How about you and Lily, Essie?

MRS. MILLER. Well, I thought we'd just sit around and rest and talk.

MILLER. You can gossip any day. (MILDRED, *slight*

*snicker.* SID *chuckles.)* This is the Fourth. Now. I've got a better suggestion than that. (EVERYONE *interested. A step in for* SID.) What do you say to an automobile ride? I'll get out the Buick and we'll drive around town and out to the lighthouse and back. Then Sid and I will let you off here, or anywhere you say, and we'll go on to the picnic.

MRS. MILLER. *(Lift)* I'd love it. Wouldn't you, Lily?

LILY. *(Lift)* It would be nice.

MILLER. Then, that's all settled.

SID. *(Embarrassedly, crosses* R. *of* LILY) Lily. want to come with me to the fireworks display at the beach tonight? (MILLER *and* MRS. MILLER *exchange a glance.)*

MRS. MILLER. *(Standing* R. *of* MILLER) That's right, Sid. You take her out.

LILY. *(Flustered and grateful)* I—I'd like to, Sid. Thank you. *(Then an apprehensive look comes over her face)* Only not if you come back—you know! (MRS. MILLER *crosses to bookcase up* C.)

ARTHUR. *(With heavy jocularity—lift—quickly)* Listen, Uncle Sid. Don't let me catch you and Aunt Lily spooning on a bench tonight—or it'll be my duty to call a cop! (SID *and* LILY *look painfully embarrassed at this.* SID *crosses; sits chair up* L. *and the joke falls flat, except for* MILDRED, *who can't restrain a giggle at the thought of these two ancients spooning.)*

MRS. MILLER. *(Rebukingly)* Arthur! *(Sharply, over her shoulder.)*

MILLER. *(Dryly—overlap* MRS. MILLER'S *"Artur")* That'll do you! Kicking a football around Yale seems to have blunted your sense of humor!

MRS. MILLER. *(Faces front)* Where's Richard?

MILDRED. I'll bet he's off somewhere writing a poem to Muriel McComber, the silly! Or pretending to write one. I think he just copies—

ARTHUR. He's still in the dining-room, reading a book. Gosh, he's always reading now. It's not *my* idea of having a good time in vacation.

MRS. MILLER. *(Sharply, crosses to L. of* MILLER*)* That reminds me, Nat. I've been meaning to speak to you about those awful books Richard is reading. You've got to give him a good talking to— *(Starts off* L.C.*)* I'll go up and get them right now. I found them where he'd hid them on the shelf in his wardrobe. You just wait till you see what— *(She bustles off* L.C. SID *watches her exit.)*

MILLER. *(Plainly not relishing whatever is coming —grumblingly—rises; crosses to* SID*)* Seems to me she might wait until the Fourth is over before bringing up— *(Then with a grin)* I know there's nothing to it, anyway. Gosh, when I think of the books I used to sneak off and read when I was a kid!

SID. *(Crossses and sits chair #3; picks up paper)* Me, too. I suppose Dick is deep in "Nick Carter" or "Old Cap Collier."

MILLER. *(Crosses to L. of* SID*)* No, he passed that period long ago. Poetry's his red meat nowadays, I think— (ARTHUR *and* MILDRED *look at* MILLER) —love poetry— (MILDRED *giggles.)* And Socialism, too, I suspect, from some dire declarations he's made. (ARTHUR—*a bit of angry reaction. Then briskly— with a grin)* Well, might as well get him on the carpet. *(He calls)* Richard. *(No answer. Louder— crosses up* C.*)* Richard. *(No answer—in a bellow)* Richard!

ARTHUR. I'll get him, Pa! *(Shouting, crosses up and exits* R.C.*)* Hey, Dick, wake up! Pa's calling you.

RICHARD'S VOICE. *(From the dining room. Irritated)* All right. I'm coming.

MILLER. Darn him! *(Amused)* When he gets his nose in a book, the house could fall down and he'd never—

(RICHARD *appears in the* R.C. *doorway, the book he has been reading in one hand, a finger marking his place. He looks a bit startled still, reluctantly called back to earth from another world. He is sixteen, just out of high school. In appearance he is a perfect blend of father and mother, so much so that each is convinced he is the image of the other. He has his mother's light-brown hair, his father's gray eyes; his features are neither large nor small; he is of medium height, neither fat nor thin. One would not call him a handsome boy; neither is he homely. But he is definitely different from both of his parents, too. There is something of extreme sensitiveness added—a restless, apprehensive, defiant, shy, dreamy, self-conscious intelligence about him. In manner he is alternately plain, simple boy and a posey actor solemnly playing a role. He is dressed in prep. school reflection of the college style of* ARTHUR. ARTHUR *follows him in and remains upstage.*)

RICHARD. *(Crossing into room)* Did you want me, Pa?

MILLER. *(Dryly)* I'd hoped I'd made that plain. Come and sit down a while. *(He points to chair* #1. *As he starts down* R. MILDRED *slides to upstage end of sofa, preparing to trip him.)*

RICHARD. *(Coming forward—seizing on the opportunity to play up his preoccupation—with apologetic superiority)* I didn't hear you, Pa. *(Crosses to down* R.) I was off in another world. (MILDRED *slyly shoves her foot out so that he trips over it, almost falling. She laughs gleefully. So does* ARTHUR.)

ARTHUR. *(Crosses down a bit)* Good for you, Mid! That'll wake him up!

RICHARD. *(Grins sheepishly—all boy now)* Darn you, Mid! I'll show you! *(He pushes her back on the*

*sofa and tickles her with his free hand, still holding
the book in the other. She shrieks.)*

ARTHUR. Give it to her, Dick! (SID *enjoys tussle.)*

MILLER. That's enough now. No more roughhouse.
*(Indicates chair)* You sit down here, Richard. (MIL-
LER *stalls a little.* ARTHUR *crosses and sits upstage of*
MILDRED. RICHARD *obediently sits in chair #1.)*
What were you planning to do with yourself today?
Going out to the beach with Mildred?

RICHARD. *(Scornfully superior)* That silly skirt
party! I should say not!

MILDRED. He's not coming because Muriel isn't.
I'll bet he's got a date with her somewheres. (ARTHUR
*laughs.)*

RICHARD. *(Flushing bashfully)* You shut up, Mid!
*(Then to his father)* I thought I'd just stay home,
Pa—this morning, anyway. *(WARN Crackers—1
loud.)*

MILLER. Help Tommy set off firecrackers, eh?

RICHARD. *(Drawing himself up—with dignity)* I
should say not. *(Then frowning portentously.* SID
*looks from paper at* RICHARD) I don't beleve in this
silly celebrating the Fourth of July—all this lying
talk about liberty—when there is no liberty!

MILLER. *(A twinkle in his eye)* Hmmm.

RICHARD. *(Getting warmed up)* The land of the
free and the home of the brave! Home of the slave
is what they ought to call it—the wage slave ground
under the heel of the capitalist class, starving, crying
for bread for his children, and all he gets is a stone!
The Fourth of July is a stupid farce! (SID *and* MIL-
LER *exchange look.* SID *turns upstage and reads
paper.)*

MILLER. *(Putting a hand to his mouth to conceal
a grin)* Hmm. Them are mighty strong words. You'd
better not repeat such sentiments outside the bosom
of the family or they'll have you in jail.

SID. *(Not looking up from paper)* And throw away the key.

RICHARD. *(Darkly. Overlap cue)* Let them put me in jail. *(Lift)* But how about the freedom of speech in the Constitution, then? That must be a farce, too. *(Then he adds grimly)* No, you can celebrate your Fourth of July. I'll celebrate the day the people bring out the guillotine again and I see Pierpont Morgan being driven by in a tumbril! *(CRACKER, loud. His father and* SID *are vastly amused.* LILY *is shocked but, taking her cue from them, smiles.* MILDRED *stares at him in puzzled wonderment, never having heard this particular line before. Only* ARTHUR *betrays the outraged reaction of a patriot.)*

ARTHUR. Aw, say, you fresh kid, tie that bull outside! You ought to get a punch in the nose for talking that way on the Fourth! *(*RICHARD *looks front, so mad he can't find words.)*

MILLER. *(Solemnly—pause—amused)* Son, if I didn't know it was you talking, I'd think we had Emma Goldman with us.

ARTHUR. *(Virtuously—lift)* Never mind, Pa. Wait till we get him down to Yale. We'll take that out of him!

RICHARD. *(With high scorn)* Oh, Yale! After all what is Yale?

ARTHUR. *(Angrily)* You'll find out what!

MILLER. *(With a comic air of resignation)* Well, Richard, I've always found I've had to listen to at least one stump speech every Fourth. I only hope getting your extra strong one right after breakfast will let me off for the rest of the day. *(They* ALL *laugh now, taking this as a cue.* RICHARD, *hurt and mad, tries to read his book.)* What's that book, Richard?

RICHARD. *(Importantly, as though it were a three-word title)* Carlyle's French Revolution. *(*SID *picks up paper; begins to read, back to audience.)*

MILLER. Hmm. So that's where you drove the
tumbril from and piled poor old Pierpont in it. *(Then
seriously)* Glad you're reading it, Richard. It's a
darn fine book.

RICHARD. *(With unflattering astonishment)* What,
have you read it? (SID *and* MILLER *exchange glance.)*

MILLER. *(Apologetically)* Well, you see, even a
newspaper owner can't get out of reading a book
every now and again.

RICHARD. *(Abashed)* I—I didn't mean—I know
you— *(Then enthusiastically)* Say, isn't it a great
book, though—that part about Mirabeau—and about
Marat and Robespierre—

MRS. MILLER. *(Appears from* L.C. *in a great state
of flushed annoyance)* Never you mind Robespierre,
young man! (SID *listens to this; crosses to* L. *of chair
#2.)* You tell me this minute where you've hidden
those books! They were on the shelf in your wardrobe
and now you've gone and hid them somewheres else.
You go right up and bring them to your father.
(RICHARD, *for a second, looks suddenly guilty and
crushed. Then he bristles defensively.)*

MILLER. *(Sharply; overlap cue)* Never mind his
getting them now. We'll waste the whole morning
over those darned books. And anyway, he has a right
to keep his library to himself. *(Look from* MRS. MIL-
LER.) That is, if they're not too— *(*SID *looks over*
L. *shoulder at* MILLER.) What books are they, Richard?

RICHARD. *(Self-consciously hesitant)* Well—
there's—

MRS. MILLER. I'll tell you if he won't—and you
give him a good talking to. *(Then, after a glance at*
RICHARD) Two books were by that awful Oscar
Wilde they put in jail for heaven knows what wicked-
ness.

ARTHUR. *(Suddenly—solemnly authoritative)* He
committed bigamy. *(Then as* SID *smothers a burst*

*of ribald laughter)* What are you laughing at? I
guess I ought to know. A fellow at college told me.
His father was in England when this Wilde was
pinched—and he said he remembered once his mother
asked his father about it and he told her he'd committed bigamy.

MILLER. *(Hiding a smile behind his hand)* Well,
then, that must be right, Arthur.

MRS. MILLER. *(Lift; angrily—to* MILLER) I
wouldn't put it past him, nor anything else. One book
was poetry. "The Ballad" of I forget what.

RICHARD. *(Defiantly)* "The Ballad of Reading
Gaol," one of the greatest poems ever written. *(He
pronounces it "Reading Goal"—as in goalpost.)*

MRS. MILLER. And then there were two books by
that Bernard Shaw— You know, Nat, the one who
wrote a play—that was so vile they wouldn't even let
it play in New York!

MILLER. Hmm. I remember.

MRS. MILLER. And there was a book of plays by
that Ibsen there, too! And poems by Swin-some-
thing—

RICHARD. "Poems and Ballads by Swinburne," Ma.
The greatest poet since Shelley! *(To* MILLER) He
tells the truth about real love!

MRS. MILLER. Love! Well, all I can say is, from
reading here and there, that if he wasn't flung in jail
along with Wilde, he should have been. Some of the
things I simply couldn't read, they were so indecent.
And then there was Kipling's— *(Sits as she speaks in
chair #2)* —but I suppose he's not so bad. And last
there was a poem—a long one—the Rubay— *(Sharply)* What is it, Richard?

RICHARD. *(Front)* "The Rubaiyat of Omar Khay-
yam!" That's the best of all!

MRS. MILLER. *(Grunts)* Humph!

MILLER. Oh, I've read that, Essie.

MRS. MILLER. *(Shocked)* Why, Nat!

MILLER. Yes, got a copy down at the office now—
There's fine things in it, seems to me—true things.

MRS. MILLER. *(A bit bewildered and uncertain
now)* Why, Nat, I don't see how you—

RICHARD. *(Enthusiastically)* Gee—it's wonderful,
isn't it, Pa? Remember this? *(Then even more en-
thusiastically)*
"A Book of Verses underneath the Bough,
   A Jug of Wine, a Loaf of Bread—and Thou
   Beside me singing in the Wilderness—"

ARTHUR. *(Who, bored to death by all this poetry
quoting, looks out window down R.)* Hey, look who's
coming up the walk—Old Man McComber!

MILLER. *(Irritably)* Dave?

ARTHUR. *(Rising)* Yeah!

MILLER. Now what in thunder does that damned
old—

MRS. MILLER. *(Vexatiously. Rises)* He'll know
we're in this early, too. No use lying. *(Then appalled
by another thought)* Lily, let's us run up the back
stairs and get our things on. Nat, you get rid of him
the first second you can! Whatever can the old fool
want— *(She and LILY hurry out R.C. MILLER glances at his watch and crosses down L., then up L.)*

*(WARN Bell.)*

ARTHUR. *(Glancing at his watch)* I'm going to beat
it—just time to catch the eight-twenty trolley.

MILDRED. I've got to catch that, too. *(She rushes
off R.C.)*

ARTHUR. *(He turns at R.C. door—with a grin)*
Say, listen, Dick! McComber may be coming to see
if your intentions toward his daughter are dishonor-
able! You'd better beat it while your shoes are good!
*(He disappears through R.C. door, laughing.)*

RICHARD. *(A bit shaken, but putting on a brave
front)* Think I'm scared of him!

MILLER. *(Gazing at him—frowning)* Can't imagine
what— But it's to complain about something, I know

that. I only wish I didn't have to be pleasant with the old buzzard—but he's about the most valuable advertiser I've got.

SID. *(Sympathetically)* I know. But tell him to go to hell, anyway. He needs that ad more than you. *(The sound of the BELL comes from the rear of the house off right from back parlor.)*     *(BELL.)*

MILLER. There he is. You clear out, Dick—(RICHARD *rises.)*—but come right back as soon as he's gone, you hear? *(Lifting a little)* I'm not through with you, yet.

RICHARD. Yes, Pa. *(Crosses to door, R.C.)*

MILLER. You better clear out, too, Sid.

SID. Come on, Dick, we'll go out and help Tommy celebrate. *(He takes RICHARD'S arm and they also disappear through R.C. door. MILLER glances through the front parlor toward the front door, curses under his breath, then calls in a tone of strained heartiness.)*

MILLER. *(Upstage in view of audience but in front parlor L.C.)* Hello, Dave. *(Enters)* Come right in here. What good wind blows you around on this glorious Fourth? *(A flat, brittle voice answers him: "Good morning," and a moment later DAVID Mc-COMBER appears in the R.C. doorway. He is a thin, dried-up little man with a head too large for his body perched on a scrawny neck, and a long solemn horse face with deep-set little black eyes, a blunt formless nose and a tiny slit of a mouth. He is about the same age as MILLER but is entirely bald, and looks ten years older. He is dressed with a prim neatness in shiny old black clothes.)* Here, sit down and make yourself comfortable. *(Taking cigar case from pocket)* Have a cigar?

McCOMBER. *(Acidly. Sits chair down L.C.)* You're forgetting. I never smoke.

MILLER. *(Forcing a laugh at himself)* That's so. So I was. Well, I'll smoke alone, then. *(He bites off the end of the cigar viciously, as if he wished it were*

McComber's *head, and sits down on desk chair; faces* McComber.)

McComber. You asked me what brings me here, so I'll come to the point at once. I regret to say it's something disagreeable—disgraceful would be nearer the truth—and it concerns your son, Richard!

Miller. *(Beginning to bristle—but calmly)* Oh, come, now, Dave. I'm sure Richard hasn't—

McComber. *(Sharply)* And I'm positive he has. I have proof of everything *in his own handwriting!*

Miller. Let's get down to brass tacks. Just what is it you're charging him with?

McComber. With being dissolute and blasphemous—with deliberately attempting to corrupt the morals of my young daughter, Muriel.

Miller. Then I'm afraid I'll have to call you a liar, Dave!

McComber. *(Without taking offense—in the same flat, brittle voice)* I thought you'd get around to that, so I brought the proofs with me. *(He takes a wallet from his inside coat pocket, selects five or six slips of paper, and holds them out to* Miller*)* My wife discovered them in one of Muriel's bureau drawers, hidden under the underwear. They're all in his handwriting. You can't deny it. Anyway, Muriel's confessed to me he wrote them. You read them and then say I'm a liar. (Miller *has taken the slips and is reading them frowningly.* McComber *talks on)* Evidently you've been too busy to take the right care about Richard's bringing up or what he's allowed to read—though I can't see why his *mother* failed in her duty.

Miller. *(Has finished the last of the slips and is making a tremendous effort to control his temper)* Why, you damned old fool! Can't you see Richard's only a fool kid who's just at the stage when he's out to rebel against all authority, and so he grabs at everything radical to read and wants to pass it on to his elders and his girl and boy friends to show off what a young hellion he is! Why, at heart you'd find Richard is just as innocent and as big a kid as your Muriel is! This stuff doesn't mean anything to me— If you believe this could corrupt Muriel, then you must believe she's easily corrupted! But I'll bet you'd find she knows a lot more about life than you give her credit for—and can guess a stork didn't bring her down your chimney!

McCOMBER. Now you're insulting my daughter.

MILLER. I'm not insulting her. I'm giving her credit for ordinary good sense. I'd say the same about my own Mildred, who's the same age.

McCOMBER. I know nothing about your Mildred except that she's known all over as a flirt. *(Then more sharply)* Well, I knew you'd prove obstinate, but I certainly never *dreamed* you'd have the impudence, after reading those papers, to claim your son was innocent of all wrong-doing!

MILLER. *(Interrupts—getting sore)* No? *(He tosses slips of paper on desk)* Just what *did* you dream I'd do?

McCOMBER. Do what it's your plain duty to do as a citizen to protect other people's children! Take and give him a hiding he'd remember to the last day of his life!

MILLER. *(His fists clenched, leans toward McCOMBER)* Dave, I've stood all I can stand from you! You get out! And get out quick, if you don't want a kick in the rear to help you!

McCOMBER. *(Again in his flat, brittle voice, slowly getting to his feet but evincing no particular fear. Stands* R. *and below chair down* L.C. NAT *rises too)* You needn't lose your temper. I'm only demanding you do your duty by your own as I've already done by mine. I'm punishing Muriel. She's not to be allowed out of the house for a month and she's to be in bed every night by eight sharp. And yet she's blameless, compared to that—

MILLER. *(Crosses to him—belligerently)* I said I'd had enough out of you, Dave!

McCOMBER. *(Quickly—taking a step backward)* You needn't lay hands on me. I'm going. But there's one thing more. *(He takes a letter from his wallet)* Here's a letter from Muriel for your son. *(Hands* MILLER *the letter)* It makes clear, I think, how she's come to think about him, now that her eyes have been opened. I hope he heeds what's inside—for his own good and yours— And don't think I'm not going to make you regret the insults you've heaped on me. *(With a thin little sneer)* I'm taking the advertisement for my store out of your paper—and it won't go in again, I tell you, not unless you apologize in writing and promise to punish—

MILLER. I'll see you in hell first! As for your damned old ad, take it out and go to hell!

McCOMBER. *(Not impressed—flatly)* That's plain bluff. You know how badly you need it. So do I. Well, good day. (McCOMBER *turns and starts stiffly for door* L.C. *and exits through front parlor.* MILLER *stands looking after him. Slowly the anger drains from his face and leaves him looking a bit sick and disgusted.* MILLER *then looks at letter; puts it in pocket of coat. He crosses to desk* L. *and is picking up the slips of paper* McCOMBER *brought when* SID *enters.* SID *appears from* R.C. *His face is one broad grin of satisfaction.)*

SID. *(Enters as he speaks)* Good for you, Nat! You sure gave him hell!

MILLER. *(Dully—sits on desk chair)* Much good it'll do. He knows it was all talk.

SID. McComber never saw you like this before. I tell you you scared the pants off him. *(He chuckles; notices the slips of paper in* MILLER's *hand)* What's

this? Something he brought? *(Sits on side chair down
L.C., facing* MILLER.)

MILLER. *(Grimly)* Samples of the new freedom—
*(Gives* SID *slips of paper.* SID *reads them.)*—from
those books Essie found—that Richard's been passing on to Muriel to educate her. They're what started
the rumpus. *(Then frowning)* I've got to do something about that young anarchist or he'll be getting
me, and himself, in a peck of trouble.

SID. *(Has been reading the slips, a broad grin on
his face. Edges chair a bit toward* MILLER. *Suddenly he whistles)* Phew! This is a warm lulu for fair!
*(He recites with a joking intensity)*

"My life is bitter with thy love; thine eyes
    Blind me, thy tresses burn me, thy sharp sighs
    Divide my flesh and spirit with soft sound—"

MILLER. *(With a grim smile)* Hmm. I missed that
one. That must be Mr. Swinburne's copy. I've never
read him, but I've hear something like that was the
matter with him.

SID. Yes, it's labellel Swinburne—"Anactoria."
Whatever that is. But wait, watch and listen! The
worst is yet to come! *(He recites with added comic
intensity)*

"That I could drink thy veins as wine, and eat
    Thy breasts like honey,

(MILLER *looks at* SID, *who indicates it on paper.)*
————————— that from face to feet
    The body were abolished and consumed,
    And in my flesh thy very flesh entombed!"

MILLER. *(Takes slips, glances at them and then an
irrepressible boyish grin coming to his face)* Hell
and hallelujah! Just picture old Dave digesting that
for the first time! (BOTH *laugh)* Gosh, I'd give a
lot to have seen his face! *(Then a trace of shocked
reproof showing in his voice)* But it's no joking
matter. That stuff *is* warm—*(Puts slips on desk)*—
too damned warm, if you ask me! I don't like this a

damned bit, Sid. Don't know but what I agree with McComber. That's no kind of thing to be sending a decent girl. *(More worriedly)* I thought he was really stuck on her—as one gets stuck on a decent girl at his age—all moonshine and holding hands and a kiss now and again. But this looks—I wonder if he is hanging around her to see what he can get? *(Angrily)* By God, if that's true, he deserves that licking McComber says it's my duty to give him! I've got to draw the line somewhere!

SID. Yes, it won't do to have him getting any decent girl in trouble.

MILLER. *(Which he doesn't want to do)* The only thing I can do is put it up to him straight. *(With pride)* Richard'll stand up to his guns, no matter what. I've never known him to lie to me.

SID. *(At a noise from the back parlor, RICHARD softly calls "Uncle Sid.")* Then now's your chance. I'll beat it. (RICHARD *enters* R.C., *very evidently nervous about* McCOMBER'S *call.)*—and see if the women folks are ready upstairs. *(Lift)* We ought to get started soon—if we're ever going to make that picnic. *(Exits* L.C.*)*

RICHARD. *(Forcing a snicker—crosses to down* L.C.*)* Gee, Pa, Uncle Sid's a bigger kid than Tommy is. He was throwing firecrackers in the air and catching them.

MILLER. Never mind that. I've got something else to talk to you about besides firecrackers.

RICHARD. *(Apprehensively)* What, Pa?

MILLER. *(Rises. Suddenly puts both hands on his shoulders and looks into his eyes—quietly)* Look here, son. I'm going to ask you a question, and I want an honest answer. I warn you beforehand if the answer is "yes" I'm going to punish you and punish you hard because you'll have done something no boy of mine ought to do. But you've never lied to

me before, I know, and I don't believe, even to save
yourself punishment, you'd lie to me now, would you?

RICHARD. *(Impressed—with dignity)* I won't lie,
Pa.

MILLER. *(Slowly—becoming terribly embarrassed)*
Have you been trying to have something to do with
Muriel—something you shouldn't—you know what I
mean.

RICHARD. *(Stares at him for a moment, as if he
couldn't comprehend—then, as he does, a look of
righteous indignation comes over his face)* No!
What do you think I am, Pa? I never would! She's
not that kind! (MILLER, *satisfied, looks away from*
RICHARD) Why, I—I love her! I'm going to marry
her—after I get out of college! She's said she would!
We're engaged!

MILLER. *(A great relief showing in his face—
gently. Looks at* RICHARD, *smiles)* All right. That's
all I want to know. We won't talk any more about
it. *(He gives him an approving pat on the back.)*

RICHARD. *(Still indignant)* I don't see how you
could think— *(Glances up* L., *then to* MILLER) Did
that old idiot McComber say that about me?

MILLER. *(Joking now)* Shouldn't call your future
father-in-law names, should you? 'Tain't respectful.
*(Then after a glance at* RICHARD'S *indignant face—
he points to the slips of paper on the desk)* Well,
you can't exactly blame old Dave, can you, when you
read through that literature you wished on his innocent daughter?

RICHARD. *(Crosses to desk. Sees the slips for the
first time and is overcome by embarrassment, which
he immediately tries to cover up with a superior, airy
carelessness)* Oh, so that's why. He found those,
did he? *(Puts them in pocket)* I told her to be careful— *(Drops one; picks it up; puts it in pants pocket)*
Well, it'll do him good to read the truth about life
for once and get rid of his old-fogey ideas.

MILLER. *(Growing nervous again)* I'm afraid I've got to agree with him, though, that they're hardly fit reading for a young girl. *(Then with subtle flattery)* They're all well enough, in their way, for you who're a man—*(An unconscious agreement from* RICHARD.*)* but— Think it over, and see if you don't agree with me.

RICHARD. *(Embarrassedly, but not ashamed)* Aw, I only did it because I liked them—*(Crosses to* L. *of* MILLER*)*—and I wanted her to face life as it is. She's so darned afraid of life—afraid of her Old Man— afraid of people saying this or that about her—afraid of being in love—afraid of everything. She's even afraid to let me kiss her. I thought, maybe, reading those things—they're beautiful, aren't they, Pa?

MILLER. *(Amused—but trying not to show it)* Hmmm!

RICHARD. I thought they would give her the spunk to lead her own life, and not be—always thinking of being afraid.

MILLER. I see. Well, I'm afraid she's still afraid. *(Takes the letter from the table)* Here's a letter from her he said to give you. (RICHARD *takes the letter from him uncertainly, his expression changing to one of apprehension.* MILLER *adds with a kindly smile)* You better be prepared for a bit of a blow. But never mind, son. There's lots of other fish in the sea. (RICHARD *is not listening to him, but staring at the letter with a sort of fascinated dread.* MILLER *looks into his son's face a second, then turns away, troubled and embarrassed)* Darn it! *(Lift)* I better go up-stairs and get rigged out or I never will get to that picnic. *(He moves awkwardly and self-consciously off* L.C.*)*

RICHARD. *(Continues to stare at the letter for a moment, then sits in chair down* L.C.—*then girds up his courage and tears it open and begins to read*
                    *(WARN Curtain.)*

*swiftly. As he reads his face grows more and more wounded and tragic, until at the end his mouth draws down at the corners, as if he were about to break into tears. With an effort he forces them back and his face grows flushed with humiliation and wronged anger. Blurts out to himself)* The little coward! I hate her! She can't treat me like that! I'll show her!

MRS. MILLER. *(Off stage)* Sid, don't forget your goggles.

SID. *(Off stage)* I won't. *(At sound of VOICES from off* L.C., RICHARD *quickly shoves the letter into the inside pocket of his coat and does his best to appear calm and indifferent, even attempting to whistle "Waiting at the Church." But the whistle peters out miserably as his mother,* LILY *and* SID *enter* L.C. LILY *crosses to table* C., SID *to door up* L. MRS. MILLER *crosses to* RICHARD. *They are dressed in all the elaborate paraphernalia of motoring at that period—linen dusters, veils, goggles,* SID *in a snappy cap.)*    *(WARN Cracker.)*

MRS. MILLER. *(Very chatty)* Well, we're about ready to start at last, thank goodness! Let's hope no more callers are on the way. What did that McComber want, Richard, do you know? Sid couldn't tell us.

RICHARD. You can search me. Ask Pa. *(*SID *crosses to* LILY; *helps her into coat.* LILY *ad libs. "Thank you, Sid.")*

MRS. MILLER. *(Immediately sensing something "down" in his manner—going to him worriedly)* Why, whatever's the matter with you, Richard? You sound as if you'd lost your last friend! What is it?

RICHARD. *(Desperately)* I—I don't feel so well— my stomach's sick.

MRS. MILLER. *(Immediately all sympathy, smoothing his hair back from his forehead)* You poor boy! *(*RICHARD *pulls away.)* What a shame—on the Fourth, too, of all days! *(Turning to the* OTHERS*)* Maybe I better stay home with him, if he's sick.

LILY. Yes, I'll stay, too. Poor boy!

RICHARD. *(More desperately)* No! You go, Ma! I'm not really sick. I'll be all right. You go. I want to be alone! *(Then, as a louder BANG comes from in back as* TOMMY *sets off a cannon cracker, he jumps to his feet)* Darn Tommy and his darned firecrackers. You can't get any peace in this house with that darned kid around! *(Crosses to down* C.*)* Darn the Fourth of July, anyway! *(Crosses up* L.*)* I wish we still belonged to England!         *(Loud CRACKER.)*

## FAST CURTAIN

## ACT ONE

### SCENE II

*Dining-room of the Miller home—a little after six in the evening of the same day.*

> NOTE: *This scene can be played in the Scene One setting, and the entrances can be arranged accordingly.*

*The room is much too small for the medium-priced, formidable dining-room set, especially now when all the leaves of the table are in. At Right, toward rear, is a double doorway with sliding doors and portieres leading into the back parlor. In the rear wall, Right Center, is the door to the pantry. At the Left of door is the china closet with its display of the family cut glass and fancy china. In the Left wall are two windows looking out on a side lawn. In front of the windows is a heavy, ugly side-board with three pieces of old silver on its top. In the Right wall, down stage, is a* **screen** *door opening on a side porch. A* **dark** *rug covers most of the floor. The table, with a chair at each end, Left and Right, three chairs on the far side, facing front, and two on the near side, their backs to front, takes up most of the available space. The walls are papered in a sombre brown and dark-red design. The chairs are numbered from one to seven to simplify direction. Armchair right end of table is #1—side chair above table and Right is #2—side chair Center and above table is #3—side chair above and Left is #4—armchair at Left end of table is #5—side chair below and Left is #6—side chair below and Right is #7.*

(MRS. MILLER *is supervising and helping the Second Girl,* NORAH, *in the setting of the table.* NORAH *is a clumsy, heavy-handed, heavy-footed, long-jawed, beamingly good-natured young Irish girl—a "greenhorn."* NORAH *down stage back to audience.* MRS. MILLER *Right of table shining glass with a cloth.*)

MRS. MILLER. I really think you better put on the lights, Norah. It's getting so cloudy out, and this pesky room is so dark anyway.

NORAH. Yes, Mum. *(She stretches awkwardly over the table to reach the chandelier that is suspended from the middle of the ceiling and manages to turn one LIGHT on—scornfully)* Arrah, the contraption!                    *(LIGHT.)*

MRS. MILLER. *(Worriedly)* Careful!

NORAH. *(Cheerfully)* Careful as can be, Mum. *(But in drawing back to move around to reach the next bulb she knocks against the table, pushing it upstage.)*

MRS. MILLER. *(Vexatiously crosses to* R. *end of table)* There! I do wish you'd watch—!

NORAH. *(A flustered appeal in her voice)* Arrah, what have I done wrong now?

MRS. MILLER. *(Draws a deep breath—then sighs helplessly)* Oh, nothing. Never mind the rest of the lights. You might as well go out in the kitchen and wait until I ring.

NORAH. *(Relieved and cheerful again)* Yes, Mum. *(She starts for the pantry.)*

MRS. MILLER. But there's one thing— *(Sits chair #7. Lets this pass helplessly—wearily)* —no, two other things—things I've told you over and over. Don't pass the plates on the wrong side at dinner tonight, and do be careful not to let that pantry door slam behind you.

NORAH. Yes, Mum. *(She goes into the pantry and lets the door almost slam behind her, but catches it in time to prevent the slam. She grins a pleased smile at* MRS. MILLER *as she allows the door to close quietly.* MRS. MILLER *sighs and reaches up with difficulty; can't reach lights. As she is doing so,* LILY *enters* R.2.*)*

LILY. Here, let me do that, Essie. I'm taller. *(As she quickly crosses to between chairs #6 and 7 and turns on ONE LIGHT.)*

MRS. MILLER. *(Gratefully, crosses to* L. *of chair #6)* Thank you, Lily.

LILY. *(Crosses to above table and turns on other TWO LIGHTS of chandelier)* But where's Norah? Why didn't she—?

MRS. MILLER. *(Exasperatedly crosses to between chairs #6 and 7)* Oh, that girl! She'll be the death of me! She's that thick, you honestly wouldn't believe it possible. *(Then kindly.)*

LILY. Is there anything I can do, Essie?

MRS. MILLER. *(Surveying the table. Below table* L. *to* R.*)* She's got the table all wrong. We'll have to reset it. But you're always helping me. It isn't fair to ask you—in your vacation.

LILY. *(Beginning to help with the table. Above table R. to L.)* You know I love to help. It makes me feel I'm some use in this house instead of just sponging—

MRS. MILLER. *(Indignantly, scolding—slams down fork, then speaks)* Sponging! You pay, don't you?

LILY. Almost nothing. And you and Nat only take that little to make me feel better about living with you. *(Forcing a pitiful attempt at a smile to her lips, works to below table at L. end)* I don't see how you stand me—having a cranky old-maid around all the time.

MRS. MILLER. *(Indignantly)* What nonsense you talk! As if Nat and I—weren't only too tickled to death to have you! Lily Miller, I've no patience with you when you go on like that. *(Then she changes the subject abruptly)* What time's it getting to be?

LILY. *(Glances at the little watch pinned on the bosom of her dress. She crosses from L. of table to down R.; glances off through door)* Quarter past six.

MRS. MILLER. I do hope those men folks aren't going to be late for dinner— *(She sighs; sets chairs)* But I suppose with that darned *Sachem* Club picnic it's more likely than not. (LILY *looks sad and worried, and sighs.* MRS. MILLER *gives her a quick side glance)* I see you've got your new dress on.

LILY. *(Embarrassedly. Crosses to chair #1 and sits)* Yes, I thought—if Sid's taking me to the fireworks—I ought to spruce up a little.

MRS. MILLER. *(Looking away)* Hmm. *(A pause. Then she says with an effort to be casual)* You mustn't mind if Sid comes home feeling a bit—gay. I expect Nat to and we'll have to listen to all those old stories about when he was a boy. You know what those picnics are, and he'd be running into all his old friends.

LILY. *(Agitatedly)* I don't think he will—this time—not after his promise.

MRS. MILLER. *(Avoiding looking at her)* I know.
But men are weak. *(Then quickly working to* C. *of
table, below it)* That was a good notion of Nat's,
getting Sid the job on the *Waterbury Standard*. All
Sid's ever needed was to get away from the rut he
was in here. He's the kind that's the victim of his
friends. (LILY *keeps silent, her eyes downcast.* MRS.
MILLER *goes on meaningly)* He's making good money
in Waterbury, too—thirty-five a week. He's in a
better position to get married than he ever was.

LILY. *(Stiffly)* Well, I hope he finds a woman
who's willing—though after he's through with his
betting on horse races, and dice, and playing Kelly
pool, there won't be much left for a wife—even if
there was nothing else he spent his money on.

MRS. MILLER. Oh, he'd give up all that—for the
right woman. *(Suddenly she comes directly to the
point, sharply. Sits chair #7, faces* LILY, *then speaks)*
Lily, why don't you change your mind and marry
Sid and reform him? He loves you and always has.

LILY. Never enough to stop drinking for. *(Cut-
ing off* MRS. MILLER'S *reply)* No, it's no good in
your talking, Essie. We've been over this a thousand
times before and I'll always feel the same as long as
Sid's the same. If he gave me proof he'd—but even
then I don't believe I could. It's sixteen years since
I broke off our engagement, but what made me break
it off is as clear to me today as it was then—his taking
up with bad women—

MRS. MILLER. *(Protests half-heartedly)* But he's
always sworn he got raked into that party and never
had anything to do with those harlots.

LILY. *(Firmly but quietly and quickly)* Well, I
don't believe him—didn't then and don't now. I don't
believe he deliberately planned to, but— *(Very prim)*
Oh, it's no good talking, Essie. What's done is done.
But you know how much I like Sid—in spite of
everything. I know he was just born to be what he is

—irresponsible. But don't talk to me about marry-
ing him—because I never could.

MRS. MILLER. *(Angrily front)* He's a dumb fool
—a stupid dumb fool, that's wnat he is! *(Fuming)*
It's a shame for you—a measly shame—

LILY. *(Affectionately but sharply)* Now don't you
go feeling sorry for me.

MRS. MILLER. Good gracious, if I'm not forgetting
one of the most important things! I've got to warn
that Tommy not to give me away to Nat about the
fish. He knows, because I had to send him to market
for it, and he's liable ot burst out laughing—

LILY. About what?

MRS. MILLER. *(Guiltily. Quickly)* Well, I've never
told you, but you know how Nat carries on about not
being able to eat bluefish.

LILY. *(Quickly)* I know he says it poisons him.

MRS. MILLER. *(Chuckling)* Poisons him, nothing!
He's been eating bluefish for years—only I tell him
each time it's weakfish. We're having it tonight.

LILY. *(Laughing)* Aren't you ashamed, Essie?

MRS. MILLER. Not much, I'm not. I like bluefish.
*(She laughs; rises)* Where is Tommy? In the sitting-
room? *(Crosses to R.2.)*

LILY. No, Richard's there alone. I think Tommy's
out on the piazza with Mildred. (MRS. MILLER *bustles
out* R.2. *As soon as she is gone, the smile fades from*
LILY's *lips. Her face grows sad and she again glances
nervously at her watch.* RICHARD *appears from* R.2,
*moving quickly toward door* R.1. *His face wears a
set expression of bitter gloom; he exudes tragedy.
For* RICHARD, *after his first outburst of grief and
humiliation, has begun to take a masochistic satisfaction in his great sorrow, especially in the concern
which it arouses in the family circle.)* Feel any better,
Richard?

RICHARD. *(On seeing his aunt, he gives her a dark
look and turns and crosses slowly to down* C. *Som-*

*berly—crossing down* R.) I'm all right, Aunt Lily. You mustn't worry about me.

LILY. *(Going to him—worriedly)* But I do worry about you. I hate to see you so upset.

RICHARD. *(Crosses to down* C.) It doesn't matter. Nothing matters.

LILY. *(Puts her arm around him sympathetically. He takes a step. She goes with him)* You really mustn't let yourself take it so seriously. You know, things like that come up, and we think there's no hope—

RICHARD. *(Breaks away to down* L.) Things like what come up?

LILY. What's happened between you and Muriel.

RICHARD. *(With disdain—quickly—a step down stage)* Oh, her! I wasn't even thinking about her. *(Impressively)* I was thinking about life.

LILY. *(No tenderness—a bit brittle. Crosses to a step above him)* But then—if we really, really love —why, then something else is bound to happen soon that changes everything again, and it's all as it was before the misunderstanding, and everything works out all right in the end. That's the way it is with life.

RICHARD. *(With a tragic sneer—sits chair down* L.) *Life!* Life is a *joke!* And everything works out all wrong in the end.

LILY. *(A little shocked—crosses to him)* You mustn't talk that way. *(Crosses to chair #5 and sits)* But I know you don't mean it.

RICHARD. *(Bitterly)* I do too mean it! (LILY *faces him.)* You can have your silly optimism, if you like, Aunt Lily. But don't ask me to be so blind. *(Proudly)* I'm a *pessimist!* *(Then with an air of cruel cynicism)* As for Muriel, that's all dead and past. I was only kidding her, anyway, just to have a little fun, and she took it seriously, like a fool. *(Pauses. He forces a cruel smile to his lips—rises and crosses to* L. *of* LILY*)* You know what they say about women and

trolley cars, Aunt Lily: *(Snaps finger)* There's always another one along in a minute. *(Returns and
sits down* L., *legs crossed.)*

LILY. *(Really shocked this time. Scolds)* I don't
like you when you say such horrible, cynical things.
It isn't nice.

RICHARD. Nice! *(Dislikes word "nice")* That's all
you women think of! *(Front)* I'm *proud* to be a
cynic. *(Uncrosses legs)* It's the only thing you can be
when you really face life. I suppose you think I ought
to be heartbroken about Muriel—a little coward
that's afraid to say her soul's her own, and keeps
tied to her father's apron strings! Well, not for mine!
There's plenty of other fish in the sea! *(As he is finishing,* MRS. MILLER *comes back,* R.2.)

MRS. MILLER. *(Crossing to down* C.) Why, hello.
You here, Richard? Getting hungry, I suppose?

RICHARD. *(Indignantly faces her)* I'm not hungry
a bit! That's all you think of, Ma—food! *(Faces
front.)*

MRS. MILLER. *(Dryly, crosses to below chair #6)*
Well, I must say I've never noticed you to hang
back at meal times. *(To* LILY) What's that he was
saying about fish in the sea?

LILY. *(Smiling)* He says he's through with Muriel
now.

MRS. MILLER. *(Tartly—giving her son a rebuking
look)* She's through with him, he means! The idea
of your sending a nice girl like her things out of those
indecent books! Well, nothing to do now till those
men turn up. We might as well go in the sitting room
and be comfortable. *(Starts for door* R.2.)

LILY. *(The nervous, worried note in her voice
again)* Yes, we might as well. *(They go out* R.2.)

RICHARD. *(Looking after them)* Food! *(He rises
and comes nearer the table and surveys it, especially
the cut-glass dish containing olives, with contempt
and mutters disdainfully. But the dish of olives*

*seems to fascinate him and presently he has approached nearer, and stealthily lifts a couple and crams them into his mouth. He is just reaching out for more when—)*

(WINT *whistles twice.*)

*(A low WHISTLE comes from just outside the porch door. He starts. Then a masculine voice calls, "Hey, Dick." He goes over to the screen door grumpily. Then as he recognizes the owner of the voice, his own as he answers becomes respectful and admiring. Opens door.)*

RICHARD. Oh, hello, Wint. Come on in.

*(He opens the door and WINT SELBY enters and crosses to down R.C. WINT is nineteen, a classmate of ARTHUR'S at Yale. He is a typical, good-looking college boy of the period, not the athletic but the hell-raising sport type. He is tall, blond, dressed in extreme collegiate cut. RICHARD crosses quickly to L. of WINT.)*

WINT. *(As he enters—warningly, in a low tone)* Keep it quiet, kid. I don't want the folks to know I'm here. Tell Art I want to see him a second—on the Q.T.

RICHARD. Can't. He's up at the Rands'—won't be home before ten, anyway.

WINT. *(Irritably)* Damn, I thought he'd be here for dinner. *(More irritably)* Well, that balls up things for fair!

RICHARD. *(Ingratiatingly)* What is it, Wint? Can't I help?

WINT. *(Gives him an appraising glance, hands in pockets)* I might tell you, if you can keep your face shut.

RICHARD. *(Hands in pockets, copying WINT)* I can.

WINT. *(Glances up* R. *and up* R.C.) Well, I ran into a couple of swift babies from New Haven this after and I dated them up for tonight, thinking I could catch Art— But now it's too late to get anyone else and I'll have to pass it up. I'm nearly broke and I can't afford to blow them both to drinks.

RICHARD. *(With shy eagerness, quickly)* I've got eleven dollars saved up. I could loan you some.

WINT. *(Surveys him appreciatively; pats him on back)* Say, you're a good sport. *(Then shaking his head)* Nix, Kid, I don't want to borrow your money. *(Then getting an idea)* But say, have you got anything on for tonight?

RICHARD. *(Hesitates a moment—then determinedly)* No.

WINT. Want to come along with me? *(Then quickly, but genuinely)* I'm not trying to lead you astray, understand, but it'll be a help if you would just *sit around* with Belle and feed her a few drinks while I'm off with Edith. *(He winks)* See what I mean? *(Little embarrassed, but speaks quickly)* You don't have to *do* anything, not even take a glass of beer—unless you want to.

RICHARD. *(Boastfully)* Aw, what do you think I am—a rube?

WINT. You mean you're game for anything that's doing?

RICHARD. Sure I am!

WINT. Ever been out with any girls—I mean— *(Glances about)*—real swift ones that there's something doing with, not these dead Janes around here?

RICHARD. *(Lies boldly)* Aw, what do you think? Sure I have!

WINT. Ever *drink* anything besides *sodas?*

RICHARD. Sure. Lots of times. Beer and sloe-gin fizz and—Manhattans.

WINT. *(Impressed, slaps him on back)* Hell, you know more than I thought. *(Then considering "Plot," glances* R.) Can you fix it so your folks won't get wise? *(Puts his left arm about* RICHARD'S *shoulder)* You can get back by half-past ten or eleven, though, all right. Think you can cook up some lie to cover that? *(As* RICHARD *hesitates—encouraging him)* Ought to be easy—on the Fourth.

RICHARD. Sure. Don't worry about that.

WINT. *(Pause)* But you've got to keep your face closed about this, you hear? I tell you straight, I wouldn't ask you to come if I wasn't in a hole—and if I didn't know you were coming down to *Yale* next year, and didn't think you're giving me the straight goods about having been around before. I don't want to lead you astray.

RICHARD. *(Scornfully—front)* Aw, I told you that was silly.

WINT. Well, you be at the Pleasant Beach House at half-past nine, then— (RICHARD *looks up.)* Come in the back room. And don't forget to grab some cloves to take the booze off your breath.

RICHARD. Aw, I know what to do.

WINT. *(Lift)* See you later, then. *(Shakes hands. He starts out* R.1 *and is just about to close the door when he thinks of something; turns.* RICHARD *sticks his hand out to shake hands again.)* And say, I'll say you're a *Harvard* freshman, and you back me up. They don't know a damn thing about Harvard. I don't want them thinking I'm travelling around with any high-school kid.

RICHARD. Sure. I'll fool them. That's easy.

WINT. So long, then. *(Shakes hands)* You better beat it right after your dinner while you've got a chance—and hang around until it's time. Watch your step, kid.

RICHARD. So long. *(The* R.1 *door closes behind* WINT, *who can be heard whistling.* RICHARD *stands for a moment, a look of bitter, defiant rebellion coming over his face, and mutters to himself after whistle stops)* I'll show her she can't treat me the way she's done! I'll show them all! *(Crosses and sits chair #1.)*

TOMMY. *(A moment later, rushes in R.2)* Where's Ma? *(In doorway.)*

RICHARD. *(Surlily)* In the sitting-room. Where did you think, *Bonehead?*

TOMMY. *(Crosses to R. of RICHARD)* Pa and Uncle Sid are coming. Mid and I saw them from the front piazza. Gee, I'm glad. *(Stands rear chair #6)* I'm awful hungry, ain't you? Ma! They're coming! Let's have dinner quick! *(A moment later, MRS. MILLER appears R.2 with a bowl of daisies.)* Gee, but I'm awful hungry, Ma!

MRS. MILLER. *(Crosses to above table; puts bowl of daisies on C. of table)* I know. You always are. You've got a tapeworm, that's what I think.

TOMMY. Have we got lobsters, Ma? Gee, I love lobsters

MRS. MILLER. Yes, we've got lobsters. And fish. You remember what I told you about that fish. *(He snickers.)* Now—do be quiet, Tommy! (LILY *appears* R.2, *nervous and apprehensive. As she does so, from the front yard* SID'S *VOICE is hear singing a bit maudlinly: "I nearly died with aggravation. Then she shook her head, looked at me and said: 'Poor John! Poor John!'"* MRS. MILLER *follows the example of the lady of the song and shakes her head forebodingly—but, so great is the comic spell for her, even in her brother's voice, a humorous smile hovers at the corners of her lips)* Mmm! Mmm! Lily, I'm afraid— *(Standing L. of chair #5.)*

LILY. *(Bitterly—crosses to rear of chair #2)* Yes, I might have known!

MILDRED. *(Runs in R.2. She is laughing to herself a bit shamefacedly. She rushes to her mother)* Ma, Uncle Sid's— *(She whispers in her ear.)*

MRS. MILLER. Never mind! You shouldn't notice such things—at your age!

TOMMY. *(Knowingly)* You needn't whisper, Mid. Think I don't know? Uncle Sid's *soused* again.

MRS. MILLER. *(Crosses to him; shakes him by the arm indignantly)* You be quiet! Did I ever! You're getting too smart! *(Gives him a push)* Sit right down and not another word out of you!

TOMMY. *(Aggrieved—rubbing his arm as he goes to his place)* Aw, Ma!

MRS. MILLER. *(Crosses to rear of chair #5)* Richard, you take your right place, and Mildred, sit down. (MRS. MILLER *crosses to pantry door)* You better, too, Lily. We'll get him right in here and get some food in him. He'll be all right then. (MRS. MILLER *opens the pantry door and calls)* Norah! (RICHARD, *preserving the pose of the bitter, disillusioned pessimist, sits down in his place in chair #3.* MILDRED *takes chair #7.* TOMMY *is at her* R. LILY *takes chair #2.* SID'S *chair is #4. While they are doing this, the front screen door is heard slamming and* MILLER'S *and* SID'S *laughing voices, raised as they come in and for a moment after, then suddenly cautiously lowered.* MRS. MILLER *goes to the entrance* R.2 *and calls peremptorily)* You come right in here! Don't stop to wash up or anything. Dinner's coming right on the table.

MILLER'S VOICE. *(Jovially, off stage)* All right, Essie. Here we are! Here we are!

MRS. MILLER. *(Goes to pantry door, opens it and calls)* All right, Norah. You can bring in the soup.

MILLER. *(Enters* R.2. *He isn't drunk by any means. He is just mellow and benignly ripened. His face is one large, smiling, happy beam of utter appreciation of life. All's right with the world, so satisfyingly right that he becomes sentimentally moved even to think of it)* Here we are, Essie! Right on the dot! Here we are! *(He pulls her to him and gives her a smacking*

*kiss on the ear as she jerks her head away.* MILDRED
*and* TOMMY *giggle.* RICHARD *holds rigidly aloof and
disdainful, his brooding gaze fixed on his plate.* LILY
*sits stiff and severe.)*

MRS. MILLER. *(Pulling away—embarrassedly, almost blushing—stands with her back to him. He is
directly* R. *of her and both are about four feet below
swing door.)* Don't, you crazy! *(Then recovering
herself—tartly, surveying him)* So I see, you're here!
And if I didn't, you've told me four times already!

MILLER. *(Beamingly)* Now, Essie, don't be critical. (NORAH *enters* R.C.) Don't be carpingly critical.
Good news can stand repeating, can't it? 'Course it
can! *(He slaps her jovially on her fat buttocks.*
TOMMY *and* MILDRED *roar with glee. And* NORAH,
*who has just entered from the pantry with a large
tureen of soup in her hands, almost drops it as she
explodes in a merry guffaw.)*

MRS. MILLER. *(Scandalized and flushed, she stalks
with stiff dignity toward her place—stands* L. *of chair
#5 and glares at* MILLER) Nat! Aren't you ashamed?

MILLER. *(Laughing, crosses down* C. *and then up
C.)* Couldn't resist it! Just simply couldn't resist it!
(NORAH, *still standing with the soup tureen held out
stiffly in front of her, again guffaws.)*

MRS. MILLER. *(Turns on her with outraged indignation)* Norah! Bring that soup here this minute!
*(Sits in her chair, #5.)*

NORAH. *(Guiltily)* Yes, Mum. *(She brings the
soup via above table to* MRS. MILLER. *As she starts
to move* MILLER *slaps her on the back.)*

MILLER. *(Jovially)* Why, hello, Norah!

MRS. MILLER. Nat!

NORAH. *(Rebuking him familiarly)* Arrah now,
don't be making me laugh and getting me into
trouble!

MRS. MILLER. Norah!

NORAH. *(A bit resentfully)* Yes, Mum. Here I

am. (NORAH *starts to put tureen on table while standing at* MRS. MILLER'S R. MRS. MILLER *mutters: "Didn't I tell you."* NORAH *crosses to* L. *of* MRS. MILLER *and puts soup tureen down with a thud in front of* MRS. MILLER *and then passes around to rear of table and squeezing with difficulty between the china closet and the backs of chairs at the rear of table.* MILLER *is watching off* R.2.)

MRS. MILLER. *(Picks up this immediately after reprimanding* NORAH) Tommy! *(Quick attack)* Stop spinning your napkin ring! (EVERYONE *looking at doors* R.2.) How often have I got to tell you? Mildred! Sit up straight in your chair! Do you want to grow up a humpback? Richard! Take your elbows off the table.

MILLER. *(Coming to his place at the head of the table, rubbing his hands together genially)* Well, well, well. Well, well, well. It's good to be home again. (NORAH *exits* R.C. *and lets the door slam with a bang behind her.)*

MRS. MILLER. *(Jumps)* Oh! *(Then exasperatedly)* Nat, I do wish you wouldn't encourage that stupid girl by talking to her, when I'm doing my best to train—

MILLER. *(Beamingly)* All right, Essie. Your word is law! *(Then laughing)* We did have the darndest fun today! And Sid was the life of that picnic! You ought to have heard him!

MRS. MILLER. *(As* NORAH *comes back with a dish of saltines—begins ladling soup into the stack of plates before her. She calls)* Sid! You come right in here! *(Then to* NORAH, *handing her a soup plate)* Here, Norah. (NORAH *begins passing soup.)* Sit down, Nat, for goodness sakes. Start eating, everybody. Don't wait for me. You know I've given up soup.

MILLER. *(Sits #1 but bends forward to call to his wife in a hoarse, confidential tone)* Essie—Sid's sort of embarrassed about coming— I mean, I'm afraid he's a little bit—not too much, you understand —but he met such a lot of friends and—well, you know. Don't pretend to notice, eh? And don't you kids, you hear! And don't you, Lily. He's scared of you. (NORAH *leaves.*)

LILY. *(With stiff meekness)* Very well, Nat.

MILLER. *(All beaming again—calls)* All right, Sid. The coast's clear. *(He begins to absorb his soup ravenously)* Good soup, Essie! Good soup!

SID. *(A moment later, makes his entrance* R.2. *He is in a condition that can best be described as blurry. He is not staggering but his movements have a hazy uncertainty about them. His shiny fat face is one broad, blurred, Puckish, naughty-boy grin; his eyes have a blurred, wondering vagueness. As he enters, he makes a solemnly intense effort to appear casual and dead, cold sober. He waves his hand aimlessly and says with a silly gravity)* Good evening. *(They* ALL *answer "Good evening," their eyes on their plates. He makes his way vaguely toward his place, chair #4, continuing his grave effort at conversation)* Beautiful evening. I never remember seeing—more beau'ful sunset. *(He bumps vaguely into* LILY'S *chair as he attempts to pass behind her— immediately he is all grotesque, grave politeness)* Sorry—sorry, Lily—deeply sorry—

LILY. *(Her eyes on her plate—stiffly)* It's all right.

SID. *(Manages to get into his chair at last. He is silent, studying his soup plate as if it were some strange enigma. Finally he looks up and regards his sister and asks with wondering amazement)* Soup?

MRS. MILLER. Of course it's soup. What did you think it was? And you hurry up and eat it.

SID. *(Again regards his soup with astonishment)* Well! *(Then suddenly)* Well, all right then! Soup be it! *(*EVERYONE *is relieved when* SID *starts to eat. He picks up his spoon and begins to eat, but after*

*two tries in which he finds it difficult definitely to lo-
cate his mouth, he addresses the spoon plaintively)*
Spoon, is this any way to treat a pal? *(Then suddenly comically angry, putting the spoon down with a
bang)* Down with spoons! *(He declaims)* "We'll
drink to the dead already, and hurrah for the next
who dies." *(Bowing solemnly to* R. *and* L.) Your
good—hic—health, ladies and gents. *(Lifts his soup
plate and starts drinking the soup.* MILLER *guffaws,
and* MILDRED *and* TOMMY *explode with laughter.
Even* RICHARD *forgets his melancholy and snickers,
and* MRS. MILLER *conceals a smile. Only* LILY *remains stiff and silent.)*

MRS. MILLER. *(With forced severity)* Sid!

SID. *(Solemnly offended, puts down plate)* Are
you—hic—publicly rebuking me before assembled—?
Isn't soup liquid? Aren't liquids drunk? What if they
are drunk? It's a good man's failing. *(Speaks to*
TOMMY) Am I right or wrong, Tommy?

MRS. MILLER. Hurry up and finish your soup, and
stop talking nonsense!

SID. *(Turning to her—again offendedly)* Oh, no,
Essie, if I ever so far forget myself as to drink a leg
of lamb, then you might have some—excuse for—
*(Picks up spoon)* Just think of wasted effort eating
soup with spoons—fifty gruelling lifts per plate—
billions of soup-eaters on globe—why, it's simply
staggering— *(Beams at* EVERYONE, *all happiness)*
Am I right, Nat?

MILLER. *(Who has been choking with laughter)*
Haw, haw! You're right, Sid.

SID. *(Peers at him blurredly and shakes his head
sadly)* Poor old Nat! Always wrong—and drunk
again, I regret to note. Sister, my heart bleeds for
you and your poor fatherless chicks! *(Pats* RICH-
ARD's *head.)*

MRS. MILLER. *(Restraining a giggle—severely)*
Sid! Do shut up for a minute! *(Speaks seriously)*

ate, *and they are passed around and* EVERYONE
*n pulling the cracked shells apart.* MRS. MIL-
*es the fish plates of* TOMMY, RICHARD, SID
*self and puts them on sideboard,* L.)
LER. *(Determining to give the conversation*
*turn, says to his daughter—serving lobster)*
good time at the beach, Mildred?
RED. Oh, fine, Pa, thanks. The water was
ful and warm.
LER. Swim far?
RED. Yes, for me. But that isn't so awful far.
LER. Well, you ought to be a good swimmer,
take after me. (MRS. MILLER *amused—real-*
*other long-winded story is coming—glances*
LER—*not reproachfully.)* I used to be a regu-
ter rat when I was a boy. I'll have to go down
beach with you one of these days—though I'd
ty, not having been in in all these years. *(The*
*scent look comes into his eyes of one about to*
*k on an oft-told tale of childhood adventure)*
now, speaking of swimming—(SID *looks at*
R)—I never go down to that beach but what
to mind the day I and Red Sisk went in swim-
there and I saved his life. *(By this time the*
LY *are beginning to exchange amused, guilty*
*s. They* ALL *know what is coming.)*
*(With a sly, blurry wink around. Dramatical-*
ha!
LLER. *(Turning on him)* What's that?
Nothing—go on swimming—don't mind me.
LLER. *(Glares at him—but immediately is over-*
*by the reminiscent mood again)* Well—Red
his father kept a blacksmith shop where the
Market is now—we kids called him Red be-
he had the darndest reddest crop of hair—
ckles) Well, as I was saying, Red and I went
ming that day. Must have been—let me see—

Pass me your soup plates, everybody. If we wait for that girl to take them, we'll be here all night. (ALL *pass up their plates, which* MRS. MILLER *stacks up and then puts on the sideboard. As she is doing this,* NORAH *appears* R.C. *with a platter of broiled fish. She is just about to place these before* MILLER *when* SID *catches her eye mistily and rises to his feet.)*

SID. *(Speaks with broad Irish accent. Raptly, rises)* Ah, Sight for Sore eyes, my beautiful Macush-la.

MRS. MILLER. Sid!

NORAH. *(Immensely pleased—gives him an arch, flirtatious glance)* Ah, sure, Mister Sid, it's you that have kissed the Blarney Stone, when you've a drop taken!

SID. My star-eyed Mavoureen!

MRS. MILLER. *(Outraged)* Norah! Put down that fish! (NORAH *puts down fish platter in front of* MIL-LER.)

LILY. *(Choking with angry shame, then turning on* SID, *furiously)* Will you please sit down and stop making a fool of yourself! (SID *gives her a hurt, mournful look and then sinks meekly down on his chair.)*

NORAH. *(Grinning cheerfully, gives* LILY *a reassuring pat on the back)* Ah, Miss Lily, don't mind him. He's only under the influence. Sure, there's no harm in him at all!

MRS. MILLER. Norah! (NORAH *exits hastily* R.C., *letting the door slam with a crash behind her. There is silence for a moment as* MILLER *serves the fish and it is passed around.* NORAH *comes back with the vegetables. Again the door slams behind her. She places vegetables for* LILY *to serve on dinner plates.)*

MILLER. *(After giving* LILY *several served plates, stops suddenly and asks his wife)* This isn't, by any chance, bluefish, is it, my dear? (TOMMY *clamps hand over his mouth.)*

MRS. MILLER. *(With a warning glance at* TOMMY) Of course not. It's weakfish. You know we never have bluefish, on account of you—

MILLER. *(Addressing the table now with the gravity of a man confessing his strange peculiarities)* Yes, I regret to say, there's a certain peculiar oil in bluefish that invariably poisons me. *(At this,* TOMMY *cannot stand it any more but explodes into laughter.* MRS. MILLER, *after a helpless glance at him, follows suit, laughs longest; then* LILY *goes off into uncontrollable, hysterical laughter, and* RICHARD *and* MILDRED *are caught in the contagion.* MILLER *looks around at them with a weak smile, his dignity now ruffled a bit)* Well, I must say I don't see what's so darned funny about my being poisoned.

SID. *(Peers around him—then with drunken cunning. Speaks sharply)* Aha! Nat, I suspect—plot! This fish looks blue to me—*(Turns over fish)*—very blue— *(He points his fork dramatically at* MRS. MILLER, *who starts to chuckle and then laughs)* Look how guilty *she* looks—a veritable Lucretia Borgia! Can it be this woman has been slowly poisoning you all these years? And how well—you've stood it! *(*EVERYONE *goes off into uncontrollable laughter.)*

MILLER. *(Grumpily)* Oh, give us a rest, you darned fool! *(*EVERYONE *quickly silent except* TOMMY. MILLER *glares at him. He stops.)* A joke's a joke, but— *(He addresses his wife in a wounded tone)* Is this true, Essie?

MRS. MILLER. *(Wiping the tears from her eyes— defiantly. Starts laughing again)* Yes, it is true, if you must know, and you'd never have suspected it if it weren't for that darned Tommy and Sid poking his nose in. You've eaten bluefish for years and thrived on it and it's all nonsense about that peculiar oil—

MILLER. *(Deeply offended)* Kindly allow me to

Red was fourteen, bigger and older than me. I was only twelve—forty-five years ago— Wasn't a single house down there then—but there was a stake out where the whistling buoy is now, about a mile out. (TOMMY, *who has been having difficulty restraining himself, lets out a stifled giggle.* MILLER *bends a frowning gaze on him.* MRS. MILLER *slaps* TOMMY'S *arm.)* One laugh more out of you, young man, and you'll leave the table!

MRS. MILLER. *(Quickly interposing, trying to stave off the story)* Do eat your lobster, Nat. You didn't have any fish, you know.

MILLER. *(Not liking the reminder—pettishly)* Well, if I'm going to be interrupted every second anyway— Well, as I was saying, there was I and Red, and he dared me to race him out to the stake and back. Well, I didn't let anyone dare me in those days. I was a spunky kid. So I said "all right" and we started out. We swam and swam and were pretty evenly matched; though, as I've said, he was bigger and older than me, but finally I drew ahead. *(Looks at* SID, *almost daring him to interrupt)* I was going along easy, with lots in reserve, not a bit tired, when suddenly I heard a sort of gasp from behind me—like this—"help." *(He imitates.* EVERYONE'S *eyes are firmly fixed on their plates, except* SID'S. SID *is peering at him with bleary curiosity. He puts right elbow on table.* EVERYONE *leans over their plates in attempt to keep from laughing.)* And I turned and there was Red, his face all pinched and white, and he says meekly: "Help, Nat! I got a cramp in my leg!" Well, I don't mind telling you I go mighty scared. Then suddenly I thought of the pile. If I could pull him to that, I could hang on to him till someone'd notice us. But the pile was still—well, I calculate it must have been two hundred feet away.

SID. *(Suddenly)* Two hundred and fifty! (EVERYONE *laughs.)*

MILLER. *(In confusion)* What's that?

SID. I've taken down the distance every time you've saved Red's life for thirty years and the mean average to that pile is two hundred and fifty feet! *(There is a burst of laughter from around the table.* SID *continues complainingly)* Why didn't you let that Red drown, anyway, Nat? I never knew him but I know I'd never have liked him. *(Laugh.)*

MILLER. *(Really hurt, forces a feeble smile to his lips and pretends to be a good sport about it)* Well, guess you're right, Sid. Guess I have told that one too many times and bored everyone. But it's a good true story for kids because it illustrates the danger of being foolhardy in the water—

MRS. MILLER. *(Sensing the hurt in his tone, comes to his rescue)* Of course it's a good story—and you tell it whenever you've a mind to! *(Scold sharply)* And you, Sid, if you were in any responsible state, I'd give you a good piece of my mind for teasing Nat like that!

MILLER. *(With a sad, self-pitying smile at his wife)* Getting old, I guess, Mother—getting to repeat myself. *Someone* ought to stop me.

MRS. MILLER. No such thing! You're as young as you ever were to hear you tell it. *(She turns on* SID *again angrily)* You eat your lobster and maybe it'll keep your mouth shut!

SID. *(Irrepressibly)* Lobster! Did you know, Tommy, your Uncle Sid is the man invented lobster? Fact! One day—took a day off and just dashed off lobster. *(To* MILLER*)* He was bigger'n older than me and had the darndest crop of red hair, but I dashed him off just the same! Am I right, Nat?

MRS. MILLER. Mercy sakes! Can't you shut up? *(*SID *eats lobster.)*

TOMMY. *(Suddenly in a hoarse whisper to his mother, with an awed glance of admiration at his uncle)* Ma! Look at him! He's eating that lobster, shells and all!

MRS. MILLER. *(Horrified)* Sid, do you want to kill yourself? Put that down!

SID. *(With great dignity)* But I prefer the shells. All famous epicures prefer the shells—it's the same with clams. (MILLER *howls.*) Unless I eat the shells— (SID *looks at* MILLER)—there is a certain, peculiar oil—(MILLER *stops laughing.*)—that invariably poisons me! (EVERYONE *laughs.*) Am I right, Nat?

MILLER. *(Good-naturedly)* You seem to be getting a lot of fun kidding me. *(Chuckles)* Go ahead, then. I don't mind.

MRS. MILLER. He better go right up to bed for a while, that's what he better do.

SID. *(Considering this owlishly)* Bed? Yes, maybe you're right. *(He gets to his feet. To* MRS. MILLER*)* I am not at all well—in very delicate condition. We are praying for a boy. Am I right, Nattie? *(They are again* ALL *laughing.)*

MRS. MILLER. *(Struggling with her laughter)* Will you get to bed, you idiot!

SID. *(Mutters graciously)* Immediately—if not sooner. *(He crosses up* R.C. *via rear of* LILY *and* RICHARD. *As he is crossing he sees* LILY *and speaks dramatically to no one in particular and continues his cross to above and* R. *of* LILY*)* But wait. There is still a duty I must perform. No day is complete without. *(Stoops down so his head is same height as hers—stoops to* R. *of her)* Lily, answer once and for all, will you marry me?

LILY. *(With an hysterical giggle)* No, I won't—never!

SID. *(Nodding his head, straightens up and backs up to above and* R. *of* MILLER*)* Right! And perhaps it's all for the best. For how could I forget the pre— hic—precepts taught me at mother's dying knee.

"Sidney," she said, "Sidney, my boy! Never marry a woman who drinks! Lips that touch liquor shall never touch yours!" *(Gazing at her mournfully.)*

MRS. MILLER. *(Again struggling with her laughter)* You leave Lily alone and go to bed!

SID. Right! Good night, ladies—*and* gents— We will meet—bye and bye! *(He gives an imitation of a Salvation Army drum)* Boom! Boom! Boom! Come and be saved, Brothers! *(He starts to sing the old Army hymn)* "In the sweet— Boom! Boom! *(He turns and marches solemnly out* R.2, *singing)* Bye and bye— Boom! Boom!

We will meet on that beautiful shore. Boom! Boom! Work and pray— Boom! Boom!

While you may. Boom! Boom!

We will meet in the sky bye and bye."

(MILLER *and his wife and the kids are* ALL *roaring with laughter.* LILY *giggles hysterically.)*

MILLER. *(Subsiding at last)* Haw, haw. He's a case, if ever there was one! Darned if you can help laughing at him—even when he's poking fun at you!

MRS. MILLER. Goodness, but he's a caution! Oh, my sides ache, I declare. But I suppose we really shouldn't. It only encourages him. But my lands—!

LILY. *(Suddenly gets up from her chair and stands rigidly, her face working—jerkily)* That's just it— you shouldn't—even I laughed—it does encourage— that's been his downfall—everyone always laughing, everyone always saying what a card he is, what a case, what a caution, so funny—and he's gone on— and we're all responsible—making it easy for him— and all we do is laugh! (RICHARD *turns and looks at* LILY.)

MILLER. *(Worriedly)* Now, Lily, now, you mustn't take on so! It isn't as serious as all that!

LILY. *(Bitterly)* Maybe—it is—to me. Or was— once. *(Then she says contritely)* I'm sorry, Nat.

Pass me your soup plates, everybody. If we wait for that girl to take them, we'll be here all night. (ALL *pass up their plates, which* MRS. MILLER *stacks up and then puts on the sideboard. As she is doing this,* NORAH *appears* R.C. *with a platter of broiled fish. She is just about to place these before* MILLER *when* SID *catches her eye mistily and rises to his feet.*)

SID. (*Speaks with broad Irish accent. Raptly, rises*) Ah, Sight for Sore eyes, my beautiful Macushla.

MRS. MILLER. Sid!

NORAH. (*Immensely pleased—gives him an arch, flirtatious glance*) Ah, sure, Mister Sid, it's you that have kissed the Blarney Stone, when you've a drop taken!

SID. My star-eyed Mavoureen!

MRS. MILLER. (*Outraged*) Norah! Put down that fish! (NORAH *puts down fish platter in front of* MILLER.)

LILY. (*Choking with angry shame, then turning on* SID, *furiously*) Will you please sit down and stop making a fool of yourself! (SID *gives her a hurt, mournful look and then sinks meekly down on his chair.*)

NORAH. (*Grinning cheerfully, gives* LILY *a reassuring pat on the back*) Ah, Miss Lily, don't mind him. He's only under the influence. Sure, there's no harm in him at all!

MRS. MILLER. Norah! (NORAH *exits hastily* R.C., *letting the door slam with a crash behind her. There is silence for a moment as* MILLER *serves the fish and it is passed around.* NORAH *comes back with the vegetables. Again the door slams behind her. She places vegetables for* LILY *to serve on dinner plates.*)

MILLER. (*After giving* LILY *several served plates, stops suddenly and asks his wife*) This isn't, by any chance, bluefish, is it, my dear? (TOMMY *clamps hand over his mouth.*)

MRS. MILLER. *(With a warning glance at* TOMMY*)* Of course not. It's weakfish. You know we never have bluefish, on account of you—

MILLER. *(Addressing the table now with the gravity of a man confessing his strange peculiarities)* Yes, I regret to say, there's a certain peculiar oil in bluefish that invariably poisons me. *(At this,* TOMMY *cannot stand it any more but explodes into laughter.* MRS. MILLER, *after a helpless glance at him, follows suit, laughs longest; then* LILY *goes off into uncontrollable, hysterical laughter, and* RICHARD *and* MILDRED *are caught in the contagion.* MILLER *looks around at them with a weak smile, his dignity now ruffled a bit)* Well, I must say I don't see what's so darned funny about my being poisoned.

SID. *(Peers around him—then with drunken cunning. Speaks sharply)* Aha! Nat, I suspect—plot! This fish looks blue to me—*(Turns over fish)*—very blue— *(He points his fork dramatically at* MRS. MILLER, *who starts to chuckle and then laughs)* Look how guilty *she* looks—a veritable Lucretia Borgia! Can it be this woman has been slowly poisoning you all these years? And how well—you've stood it! *(*EVERYONE *goes off into uncontrollable laughter.)*

MILLER. *(Grumpily)* Oh, give us a rest, you darned fool! *(*EVERYONE *quickly silent except* TOMMY. MILLER *glares at him. He stops.)* A joke's a joke, but— *(He addresses his wife in a wounded tone)* Is this true, Essie?

MRS. MILLER. *(Wiping the tears from her eyes— defiantly. Starts laughing again)* Yes, it is true, if you must know, and you'd never have suspected it if it weren't for that darned Tommy and Sid poking his nose in. You've eaten bluefish for years and thrived on it and it's all nonsense about that peculiar oil—

MILLER. *(Deeply offended)* Kindly allow me to

know my own constitution! (SID *nods "yes."*) Now I think of it, I've felt upset afterwards every damned timed we've had fish! *(He pushes his plate away from him with proud renunciation)* I can't eat this.

MRS. MILLER. *(Insultingly matter-of-fact)* Well, don't, then. There's lots of lobster coming and you can fill up on that. (RICHARD *suddenly bursts out laughing again.*)

MILLER. *(Turns to him, caustically)* You seem in a merry mood, Richard. Why, I thought you were the original of the Heart Bowed Down today. (RICH-*ard suddenly sobers.*)

SID. *(With mock condolence)* Never mind, Dick. Let them—scoff! *(Then with dramatic pathos, start low and build)* What do they know about girls whose hair sizzchels, whose lips are fireworks, whose eyes are red-hot sparks—

MILDRED. *(Laughing)* Is that what you wrote to Muriel? *(Turning to RICHARD)* You silly goat, you!

RICHARD. *(Surlily)* Aw, shut up, Mid. What do I care about her? *(Lift. To MRS. MILLER)* I'll show all of you how much I care! (LILY *puts hand on him. He pushes it off angrily.*)

MRS. MILLER. Pass your plates as soon as you're through, everybody. I've rung for the lobster. And that's all. You don't get any dessert or tea after lobster, you know. (NORAH *appears R.C., bearing a huge platter of cold boiled lobster which she sets before* MILLER. LILY *takes* MILLER's *plate and* MILDRED's *plate and puts them on her plate. She then picks up the fish platter so that* NORAH *can put the lobster platter down.* NORAH *then crosses to serving stand* R. *of door R.C. and leaves the fish platter and returns with the lobster plates which she puts in front of* MILLER. *She then takes the fish plates and the fish platter and exits R.C.*)

TOMMY. Gee, I love lobster! (MILLER *puts one on*

*each plate, and they are passed around and* EVERYONE
*starts in pulling the cracked shells apart.* MRS. MIL-
LER *takes the fish plates of* TOMMY, RICHARD, SID
*and herself and puts them on sideboard,* L.)

MILLER. *(Determining to give the conversation
another turn, says to his daughter—serving lobster)*
Have a good time at the beach, Mildred?

MILDRED. Oh, fine, Pa, thanks. The water was
wonderful and warm.

MILLER. Swim far?

MILDRED. Yes, for me. But that isn't so awful far.

MILLER. Well, you ought to be a good swimmer,
if you take after me. (MRS. MILLER *amused—realizes another long-winded story is coming—glances
at* MILLER—*not reproachfully.)* I used to be a regular water rat when I was a boy. I'll have to go down
to the beach with you one of these days—though I'd
be rusty, not having been in all these years. *(The
reminiscent look comes into his eyes of one about to
embark on an oft-told tale of childhood adventure)*
You know, speaking of swimming—(SID *looks at*
MILLER)—I never go down to that beach but what
it calls to mind the day I and Red Sisk went in swimming there and I saved his life. *(By this time the
FAMILY are beginning to exchange amused, guilty
glances. They* ALL *know what is coming.)*

SID. *(With a sly, blurry wink around. Dramatically)* Aha!

MILLER. *(Turning on him)* What's that?

SID. Nothing—go on swimming—don't mind me.

MILLER. *(Glares at him—but immediately is overcome by the reminiscent mood again)* Well—Red
Sisk—his father kept a blacksmith shop where the
Union Market is now—we kids called him Red because he had the darndest reddest crop of hair—
*(Chuckles)* Well, as I was saying, Red and I went
swimming that day. Must have been—let me see—

Red was fourteen, bigger and older than me. I was only twelve—forty-five years ago— Wasn't a single house down there then—but there was a stake out where the whistling buoy is now, about a mile out. (TOMMY, *who has been having difficulty restraining himself, lets out a stifled giggle.* MILLER *bends a frowning gaze on him.* MRS. MILLER *slaps* TOMMY's *arm.*) One laugh more out of you, young man, and you'll leave the table!

MRS. MILLER. *(Quickly interposing, trying to stave off the story)* Do eat your lobster, Nat. You didn't have any fish, you know.

MILLER. *(Not liking the reminder—pettishly)* Well, if I'm going to be interrupted every second anyway— Well, as I was saying, there was I and Red, and he dared me to race him out to the stake and back. Well, I didn't let anyone dare me in those days. I was a spunky kid. So I said "all right" and we started out. We swam and swam and were pretty evenly matched; though, as I've said, he was bigger and older than me, but finally I drew ahead. *(Looks at* SID, *almost daring him to interrupt)* I was going along easy, with lots in reserve, not a bit tired, when suddenly I heard a sort of gasp from behind me—like this—"help." *(He imitates.* EVERYONE's *eyes are firmly fixed on their plates, except* SID's. SID *is peering at him with bleary curiosity. He puts right elbow on table.* EVERYONE *leans over their plates in attempt to keep from laughing.)* And I turned and there was Red, his face all pinched and white, and he says meekly: "Help, Nat! I got a cramp in my leg!" Well, I don't mind telling you I go mighty scared. Then suddenly I thought of the pile. If I could pull him to that, I could hang on to him till someone'd notice us. But the pile was still—well, I calculate it must have been two hundred feet away.

SID. *(Suddenly)* Two hundred and fifty! (EVERYONE *laughs.*)

MILLER. *(In confusion)* What's that?

SID. I've taken down the distance every time you've saved Red's life for thirty years and the mean average to that pile is two hundred and fifty feet! *(There is a burst of laughter from around the table. SID continues complainingly)* Why didn't you let that Red drown, anyway, Nat? I never knew him but I know I'd never have liked him. *(Laugh.)*

MILLER. *(Really hurt, forces a feeble smile to his lips and pretends to be a good sport about it)* Well, guess you're right, Sid. Guess I have told that one too many times and bored everyone. But it's a good true story for kids because it illustrates the danger of being foolhardy in the water—

MRS. MILLER. *(Sensing the hurt in his tone, comes to his rescue)* Of course it's a good story—and you tell it whenever you've a mind to! *(Scold sharply)* And you, Sid, if you were in any responsible state, I'd give you a good piece of my mind for teasing Nat like that!

MILLER. *(With a sad, self-pitying smile at his wife)* Getting old, I guess, Mother—getting to repeat myself. *Someone* ought to stop me.

MRS. MILLER. No such thing! You're as young as you ever were to hear you tell it. *(She turns on SID again angrily)* You eat your lobster and maybe it'll keep your mouth shut!

SID. *(Irrepressibly)* Lobster! Did you know, Tommy, your Uncle Sid is the man invented lobster? Fact! One day—took a day off and just dashed off lobster. *(To MILLER)* He was bigger'n older than me and had the darndest crop of red hair, but I dashed him off just the same! Am I right, Nat?

MRS. MILLER. Mercy sakes! Can't you shut up? *(SID eats lobster.)*

TOMMY. *(Suddenly in a hoarse whisper to his mother, with an awed glance of admiration at his uncle)* Ma! Look at him! He's eating that lobster, shells and all!

MRS. MILLER. *(Horrified)* Sid, do you want to kill yourself? Put that down!

SID. *(With great dignity)* But I prefer the shells. All famous epicures prefer the shells—it's the same with clams. (MILLER *howls.*) Unless I eat the shells— (SID *looks at* MILLER)—there is a certain, peculiar oil—(MILLER *stops laughing.*)—that invariably poisons me! (EVERYONE *laughs.*) Am I right, Nat?

MILLER. *(Good-naturedly)* You seem to be getting a lot of fun kidding me. *(Chuckles)* Go ahead, then. I don't mind.

MRS. MILLER. He better go right up to bed for a while, that's what he better do.

SID. *(Considering this owlishly)* Bed? Yes, maybe you're right. *(He gets to his feet. To* MRS. MILLER*)* I am not at all well—in very delicate condition. We are praying for a boy. Am I right, Nattie? *(They are again* ALL *laughing.)*

MRS. MILLER. *(Struggling with her laughter)* Will you get to bed, you idiot!

SID. *(Mutters graciously)* Immediately—if not sooner. *(He crosses up* R.C. *via rear of* LILY *and* RICHARD. *As he is crossing he sees* LILY *and speaks dramatically to no one in particular and continues his cross to above and* R. *of* LILY*)* But wait. There is still a duty I must perform. No day is complete without. *(Stoops down so his head is same height as hers—stoops to* R. *of her)* Lily, answer once and for all, will you marry me?

LILY. *(With an hysterical giggle)* No, I won't— never!

SID. *(Nodding his head, straightens up and backs up to above and* R. *of* MILLER*)* Right! And perhaps it's all for the best. For how could I forget the pre— hic—precepts taught me at mother's dying knee.

"Sidney," she said, "Sidney, my boy! Never marry a woman who drinks! Lips that touch liquor shall never touch yours!" *(Gazing at her mournfully.)*

MRS. MILLER. *(Again struggling with her laughter)* You leave Lily alone and go to bed!

SID. Right! Good night, ladies—*and* gents— We will meet—bye and bye! *(He gives an imitation of a Salvation Army drum)* Boom! Boom! Boom! Come and be saved, Brothers! *(He starts to sing the old Army hymn)* "In the sweet— Boom! Boom! *(He turns and marches solemnly out* R.2, *singing)* Bye and bye— Boom! Boom!

We will meet on that beautiful shore. Boom! Boom!

Work and pray— Boom! Boom!

While you may. Boom! Boom!

We will meet in the sky bye and bye."

(MILLER *and his wife and the kids are* ALL *roaring with laughter.* LILY *giggles hysterically.)*

MILLER. *(Subsiding at last)* Haw, haw. He's a case, if ever there was one! Darned if you can help laughing at him—even when he's poking fun at you!

MRS. MILLER. Goodness, but he's a caution! Oh, my sides ache, I declare. But I suppose we really shouldn't. It only encourages him. But my lands—!

LILY. *(Suddenly gets up from her chair and stands rigidly, her face working—jerkily)* That's just it— you shouldn't—even I laughed—it does encourage— that's been his downfall—everyone always laughing, everyone always saying what a card he is, what a case, what a caution, so funny—and he's gone on— and we're all responsible—making it easy for him— and all we do is laugh! (RICHARD *turns and looks at* LILY.)

MILLER. *(Worriedly)* Now, Lily, now, you mustn't take on so! It isn't as serious as all that!

LILY. *(Bitterly)* Maybe—it is—to me. Or was— once. *(Then she says contritely)* I'm sorry, Nat.

I'm sorry, Essie. I didn't mean to—I'm not feeling myself tonight. If you'll excuse me. (LILY *starts for door* R.2) I'll go in the front parlor and lie down on the sofa a while.

MRS. MILLER. Of course, Lily. You do whatever you've a mind to. (LILY *goes out* R.2.)

MILLER. *(Frowning—a little shamefaced, looks after her, then to* MRS. MILLER) Hmm. I suppose she's right. Never knew Lily to come out with things that way before. Anything special happened, Essie?

MRS. MILLER. Nothing I know—except he'd promised to take her to the fireworks.

MILLER. That's so. Well, supposing I take her. I don't want her to feel disappointed.

MRS. MILLER. *(Shaking her head)* Wild horses couldn't drag her there now.

MILLER. Hmm. I thought she'd got completely over her foolishness about him long ago.

MRS. MILLER. She never will.

MILLER. She'd better. He's got fired out of that Waterbury job—

MRS. MILLER. Oh, dear—

MILLER. Told me at the picnic after he'd got enough Dutch courage in him.

MRS. MILLER. Isn't he the fool!

MILLER. I knew something was wrong when he came back home. Well, I'll find a place for him on my paper again, of course. He always was the best *news*-getter this town ever had, though you can't always print what he brought in. *(Severely)* But I'll tell him he's got to stop his damn nonsense.

MRS. MILLER. *(Doubtfully)* Yes.

MILLER. I'll tell him that. Well, no use sitting here mourning over spilt milk. *(He gets up, and* MILDRED, TOMMY *and* MRS. MILLER *follow his example. The* CHILDREN *quiet and a bit awed.)* You kids go out in the yard and try to keep quiet for a while, so's your Uncle Sid'll get to sleep and your Aunt Lily can rest.

TOMMY. *(Mournfully, crosses to* MILLER *via below table)* Ain't we going to set off the sky rockets and Roman candles, Pa?          *(WARN Curtain.)*

MILLER. Later, son, later. It isn't dark enough for them yet, anyway.

MILDRED. *(Lift. Crosses* R.*)* Come on, Tommy. I'll see he keeps quiet, Pa. (MILDRED *and* TOMMY *go out* R.I. MILLER *looks after them.)*

MILLER. That's a good girl. (RICHARD *remains sitting, sunk in bitter, gloomy thoughts.* MILLER *glances at him; crosses up* R.C.—*then a bit irritably)* Well, Melancholy Dane, what are you doing? (MRS. MILLER *is above table.)*

RICHARD. *(Darkly)* I'm going out— *(Then suddenly—lift)* Do you know what I think? It's Aunt Lily's fault Uncle Sid's going to ruin. (MILLER *and* MRS. MILLER *react to this.)* It's all because he loves her, and she keeps him dangling after her, and eggs him on and ruins his life—like all women love to ruin men's lives! I don't blame him for drinking himself to death! What does he care if he dies, after the way she's treated him! I'd do the same thing myself if I were in his boots!

MRS. MILLER. *(Indignantly)* Richard! You stop that talk!

RICHARD. *(Overlap cue. Quotes bitterly)* "Drink! For you know not whence you come nor why. Drink! For you know not why you go nor where!"

MILLER. *(Losing his temper—harshly)* Listen here, young man! I've had about all I can stand of your nonsense for one day! You're growing a lot too *big* for your size, seems to me! You keep that damn fool talk to yourself, you hear me—or you're going to regret it! Mind, now! *(He strides angrily out* R.2.*)*

MRS. MILLER. *(Still indignant)* Richard, I'm ashamed of you, that's what I am. *(She follows her husband.* RICHARD *is bitter, humiliated, wronged, even his father turned enemy, his face growing more and more rebeliious. He jumps to his feet; throws his napkin down on table.)*

RICHARD. Aw, what the hell do I care? *(Crossing to door* R. I) I'll show them! *(He turns and goes out* R. I.*)*

# FAST CURTAIN

# ACT TWO

## Scene I

*The back room of a bar in a small hotel—a small,
dingy room, dimly lighted by two fly-specked
globes in two fly-specked wall brackets Left and
Right of hall door L.C. At Right, front, is the
swinging door leading to the bar. At rear of
door, against the rear wall, is a nickel-in-the-slot
player-piano. In the rear wall, Left Center, is a
door leading to the "Family Entrance" and the
stairway to the upstairs rooms. In the Left
wall is a window with closed shutters. Three
tables with stained tops, three chairs around each
table. Table #1 is down Right—table #2 is
against rear wall just L. of piano. One chair
below this table and one L. and R. Table #3 is
up L.*

   *The hideous saffron-colored wall-paper is
blotched and spotted.*

*It is about ten the same night.*

RICHARD *and* BELLE *are discovered sitting at table
#3.* BELLE *in chair above table and* RICHARD
*in chair L. of table.*

   BELLE *is twenty, a rather pretty peroxide
blonde, a typical college "tart" of the period, and
of the cheaper variety, dressed with tawdry
flashiness. But she is a fairly recent recruit to*

*the ranks, and is still a bit remorseful behind her
make-up and defiantly careless manner.* BELLE
*has an empty gin-rickey glass before her,* RICH-
ARD *a half-empty glass of beer. He looks horribly
timid, embarrassed and guilty, but at the same
time thrilled and proud of at last mingling with
the pace that kills. The player-piano is grinding
out "Bedelia." The* BARTENDER, *a stocky young
Irishman with a foxily cunning, stupid face and
a cynically wise grin, stands just inside the bar
entrance, watching them. He is leaning on the
swinging door. The player-piano plays but one
chorus of "Bedelia" and* BELLE *sings it. The
chorus starts with the Curtain down and it raises
on word "If you'll be my Chauncy Olcott" which
is about the 8th measure of the chorus.*

BELLE. *(With an impatient glance at her escort—
rattling the ice in her empty glass)* Drink up your
beer, why don't you? It's getting flat.

RICHARD. *(Embarrassedly)* I let it get that way on
purpose. I like it better when it's flat. *(But he hastily
gulps down the rest of his glass as if it were some
nasty-tasting medicine. The* BARTENDER *chuckles
audibly.* BELLE *glances at him.)*

BELLE. *(Nodding at the player-piano scornfully)*
Say, George, is "Bedelia" the latest to hit this hick
burg? Well, it's only a couple of years old! You'll
catch up in time! Why don't you get a new roll for
that old box?

BARTENDER. *(With a grin)* Complain to the boss,
not me. We're not used to having Candy Kiddoes
like you around—or maybe we'd get up to date

BELLE. *(With a professionally arch grin at him)*
Don't kid me, please. I can't bear it. *(Then she sings
to the music from the piano, her eyes now on* RICH-
ARD) "Bedelia. I'd like to feel yer." *(The* BARTEN-

DER *laughs. She smirks at* RICHARD) Ever hear those words to it, Kid?

RICHARD. *(Who has heard them but is shocked at hearing a girl say them—putting on a blasé air)* Sure, lots of times. That's old.

BELLE. *(With a meaning smirk, edging her chair closer and putting a hand over one of his)* Then why don't you act as if you knew what they were all about?

RICHARD. *(Terribly flustered)* Sure, I've heard that old parody lots of times. *(Big Man)* What do you think I am?

BELLE. I don't know, Kid. Honest to God, you've got me guessing.

BARTENDER. *(With a mocking chuckle crossing to* R. *of table* #3) He's a hot sport, can't you tell it? I never seen such a spender. My head's dizzy bringing you in drinks!

BELLE. *(Laughs irritably—to* RICHARD) Don't let him kid you. You show him. Loosen up and buy another drink, what say?

RICHARD. *(Humiliated—manfully)* Sure. Excuse me. *(Gestures O.K. with hand)* I was thinking of something else. Have anything you like. *(He turns to the* BARTENDER) See what the lady will have—and have one on me yourself.

BARTENDER. *(Coming to the table—with a wink at* BELLE *as he picks up empty glasses)* That's talking! Didn't I say you were a sport? I'll take a cigar on you. *(To* BELLE) What's yours, Kiddo—the same?

BELLE. Yes. And forget the house rules this time and remember a rickey is supposed to have gin in it.

BARTENDER. *(Grinning)* I'll try to—seeing it's you. *(Then to* RICHARD) What's yours—another beer?

RICHARD. *(Shyly)* A small one, please. I'm not thirsty.

BELLE. *(Calculatedly taunting)* Say, honest, are

things that slow up at Harvard? Filling up on beer will only make you sleepy. Have a man's drink!

RICHARD. *(Shamefaced—weakly)* All right. I was going to. Bring me a sloe-gin fizz.

BELLE. *(To* BARTENDER*)* And make it a real one.

BARTENDER. *(With a wink)* I get you. Something that'll warm him up, eh? *(He goes into the bar.)*

BELLE. *(Looks after* BARTENDER *a moment, then at* RICHARD, *who turns front, embarrassed, and starts to whistle "Dearie."* BELLE *looks front irritably)* Christ, what a dump! (RICHARD *is startled and shocked by the curse and looks at* BELLE, *then down at the table)* If this isn't the deadest burg I ever struck! Bet they take the sidewalks in after nine o'clock. *(Then turning on him)* Say, honestly, Kid, does your mother know you're out?

RICHARD. *(Defensively)* Aw, cut it out, why don't you—trying to kid me!

BELLE. *(Glances at him—then resolves on a new tack—patting his hand)* All right. I didn't mean to, dearie. Please don't get sore at me.

RICHARD. I'm not sore.

BELLE. *(Seductively. He is not looking at her.)* You see, it's this way with me. I think you're one of the sweetest kids I've ever met—and I could like you such a lot— (RICHARD *looks front.)* —if you'd give me half a chance—*(Lift)*—instead of setting so cold and indifferent.

RICHARD. *(To* BELLE*)* I'm not cold and indifferent. *(Then solemnly tragic, turns front)* It's only that I've got—a weight on my mind.

BELLE. *(Impatiently)* Well, get it off your mind.

BARTENDER. *(Comes in, bringing the drinks; setting them down—with a wink at* BELLE*)* This'll warm him up for you. Forty cents, that is—with the cigar.

RICHARD. *(Pulls out his roll and hands a dollar bill over—with exaggerated carelessness)* Keep the change. (BELLE *emits a gasp and seems about to pro-test, then thinks better of it. The* BARTENDER *cannot believe his luck for a moment—then pockets the bill hastily, as if afraid* RICHARD *will change his mind.*)

BARTENDER. *(Respect in his voice)* Thank you very much, sir.

RICHARD. *(Grandly)* Don't mention it.

BARTENDER. *(To* RICHARD) I hope you like the drink. *(To* BELLE) I took special pains with it. *(The voice of the* SALESMAN, *who has just come in the bar, calls "Hey! Anybody here?" and a coin is rapped on the bar.*) I'm coming. *(The* BARTENDER *goes out* R.)

BELLE. *(Remonstrating gently, a new appreciation for her escort's possibilities in her voice)* You shouldn't be so generous, Dearie. Gets him in bad habits. A dime would have been plenty.

RICHARD. Ah, that's all right. I'm no tightwad.

BELLE. That's the talk I like to hear. *(With a quick look toward the bar, she stealthily pulls up her dress —to* RICHARD'S *shocked fascination—and takes a package of cheap cigarettes from her stocking)* Keep an eye out for that bartender, Kid, and tell me if you see him coming. Girls are only allowed to smoke up-stairs in the rooms, he said.

RICHARD. *(Embarrassedly, looks at her legs, then away toward* R. *door)* All right. I'll watch.

BELLE. *(Holds the package out to him)* Have a Sweet? *(Kidding him)* You *smoke*, don't you?

RICHARD. *(Taking one)* Sure! I've been smoking for the last two years—on the sly. *(She lights his cigarette, then her own and throws match on floor with elaborate nonchalance.)* But next year I'll be allowed—that is, pipes and cigars. *(He puffs but does not inhale—then, watching her with shocked concern as she inhales deeply)* Say, you oughtn't to inhale like that! Smoking's awful bad for girls, anyway, even if they don't—

BELLE. *(Cynically amused)* Afraid it will stunt my

growth? Gee, Kid, you are a scream! You'll grow
up to be a minister yet! (RICHARD *looks shamefaced.
She scans him impatiently—then pushes his drink
toward him, and holds up her drink)* Well, here's
how! Bottoms up, now! Show me you really know
how to drink. (RICHARD *follows her example and
they* BOTH *drink the whole contents of their glasses—
RICHARD longest—without setting them down.)*
There! That's something like! *(Edges her chair
toward him)* Feel better?

RICHARD. *(Proud of himself—with a shy smile.
Edges his chair a bit L. When the business is complete, the two chairs should be clear of the table)* You
bet.

BELLE. Well, you'll feel still better in a minute—
and then maybe you won't be so distant and unfriend-
ly, eh? *(Pulling up her skirts a bit.)*

RICHARD. I'm not. *(Glances at her legs.)*

BELLE. *(Teasing seductively, pats his shoulder.*
RICHARD *turns away)* Yes, you are. *(Almost pouts—
uncrosses legs)* I think you just don't like me.

RICHARD. *(More manfully)* I do too like you.

BELLE. How much? *(Crosses legs)* A lot?

RICHARD. *(Again sees legs)* Yes, a lot.

BELLE. *(Looking toward him)* Show me how
much! *(Then, as he fidgets embarrassedly, she rises
as she speaks)* Want me to come sit on your lap?

RICHARD. Yes—I— *(She comes and sits on his
lap. As he puts cigarette in cuspidor L. of him, he
looks desperately uncomfortable, but the gin is rising
to his head and he feels proud of himself and devilish,
too.)*

BELLE. Why don't you put your arm around me?
*(He does so awkwardly.)* No, not that dead way.
Hold me tight. *(Bends her head toward him as
though for a kiss.* RICHARD *draws back, scared.)*
You needn't be afraid of hurting me. I like to be
held tight, don't you?

RICHARD. Sure I do. *(Lets go of her.)*

BELLE. *(Tightening his arms about herself)* 'Specially when it's by a nice handsome kid like you. *(Ruffling his hair)* Gee, you've got pretty hair, do you know it? *(He turns front. She pulls his face to her by his hair)* Honest, I'm awfully strong for you! Why can't you be about me? *(Crosses her legs)* I'm not so awfully ugly, am I?

RICHARD. *(Sees leg)* No, you're—you're pretty.

BELLE. You don't say it as if you meant it.

RICHARD. I do mean it—honest.

BELLE. Then why don't you kiss me? *(She bends down her lips toward his. He hesitates, then kisses her a quick short peck.)* Call that kissing? Here. *(She holds his head and fastens her lips on his and holds them there. He starts and struggles, then jerks his head away. She laughs)* What's the matter, Honey Boy? Haven't you ever kissed like that before?

RICHARD. *(Front)* Sure. Lots of times.

BELLE. Then why did you jump—as if I'd bitten you? *(Squirming around on his lap)* Gee, I'm getting just crazy about you! What shall we do about it, eh? Tell me.

RICHARD. I—don't know. (BELLE *looks at him. Then boldly)* I—I'm crazy about you, too.

BELLE. *(Hugging him again. He fumbles in holding her. Speaks quietly)* Just think of the wonderful time Edith and your friend, Wint, are having—while we sit down here like two dead ones! A room only costs two dollars. *(She kisses him again, then gets up from his lap—briskly)* Come on. Go out and tell the bartender you want a room.

RICHARD. *(Starts automatically for* R. *door—then hesitates, a great struggle going on in his mind— timidity, disgust at the money element, shocked modesty, and the guilty thought of* MURIEL, *fighting it out with the growing tipsiness that makes him want to be a hell of a fellow and go in for all forbidden fruit, and makes this tart a romantic, evil vampire in his eyes. Finally, he stops and mutters in confusion)* I can't.

BELLE. *(Lift—starts for bar R. via above table #1)* What, are you too bashful to ask for a room? Let me do it, then. *(She crosses* RICHARD.*)*

RICHARD. *(Desperately, he stops her)* No—I don't want you to— *(Backs a step away from her)* I don't want to.

BELLE. *(Surveying him, anger coming into her eyes; walking toward him.* RICHARD *backs up to chair R. of table #3)* Well, if you aren't the lousiest cheap skate—

RICHARD. *(Angrily)* I'm not a cheap skate!

BELLE. *(Overlaps cue—in her anger she gets "tough")* Keep me around here all night fooling with you when I might be out with some real live one— if there is such a thing in this burg!—and now you quit on me! Don't be such a piker! You've got five dollars! I seen it when you paid for the drinks, so don't hand me any lies!

RICHARD. *(Sits chair R. of table #3; faces front)* I— Who said I hadn't? And I'm not a piker. *(Reaches for money)* If you need the five dollars so bad—you can have it without—I mean, I'll be glad to give— *(*RICHARD *has been fumbling in his pocket and pulls out his nine-dollar roll and holds out the five to her.)*

BELLE. *(Hardly able to believe her eyes, almost snatches it from his hand)* Thanks, Kid. *(Then laughs and immediately becomes sentimentally grateful)* Gee— Oh, thanks— Gee, forgive me for losing my temper and bawling you out, will you? Gee, you're a regular peach! You're the nicest kid I've ever met! *(She hugs him and he grins proudly, a hero to himself now on many counts.)*

RICHARD. *(Grandly—and quite tipsily)* It's— nothing—only too glad.

BELLE. *(Sits chair above table #3. RICHARD is in chair R. of table #3.)* Come on, let's have another drink—and this time I'll blow you just to show my appreciation. *(She calls)* Hey, George! Bring us another round—the same!

BARTENDER. *(Off stage)* Sure thing.

RICHARD. *(A remnant of caution coming to him. Scared)* I don't know as I ought to—

BELLE. Oh, another won't hurt you. And I want to blow you, see.

RICHARD. *(Boldly draws his chair closer, a bit up-stage of hers, and puts an arm around her—tipsily)* I like you a lot—now I'm getting to know you. You're a darned nice girl.

BELLE. *(Quickly)* Nice is good! Tell me another! Well, if I'm so nice, why didn't you want to take me upstairs? That's what I don't get.

RICHARD. *(Lying boldly)* I did want to—only I— *(Then he adds solemnly—big man stuff)*—I've sworn off.

BARTENDER. *(Enters R. with the drinks. Setting them on table)* Here's your pleasure. *(Then, regarding RICHARD'S arm about her waist)* Ho-ho, we're coming on, I see. (RICHARD *grins at him muzzily.* BARTENDER *holds hand out to* RICHARD.)

BELLE. *(Digs into her purse and gives him right change plus a dime tip)* Here. This is mine. (BARTENDER *goes out. She puts the five* RICHARD *has given her in her stocking and picks up her glass)* Here's how—and thanks again. *(She sips.)*

RICHARD. *(Boisterously—overlap cue)* Bottoms up! Bottoms up! *(He drinks all of his down and sighs with exaggerated satisfaction)* Gee, that's good stuff, all right.

BELLE. *(Watches him finish his drink)* What did you mean a minute ago when you said you'd sworn **off**?

RICHARD. *(Solemnly)* I took an oath I'd be faithful.

BELLE. *(Cynically)* Till death do us part, eh! *(Hastily)* Who's the girl?

RICHARD. *(Shortly, releases* BELLE*)* Never mind.

BELLE. *(Bristling)* I'm not good enough to talk about her, I suppose?

RICHARD. I didn't mean that. You're all right— *(Then with tipsy gravity)* Only you oughtn't to lead this kind of life. It isn't right—for a nice girl like you. Why don't you reform?

BELLE. *(Sharply)* Nix on that line of talk— Can it. You hear! You can do a lot with me for five dollars—but you can't reform me. See!

RICHARD. *(Rebuffed)* I—I didn't mean to hurt your feelings.

BELLE. *(Hurt, away from him)* I know you didn't mean. You're only like a lot of people who mean well, to hear them tell it. *(Changing the subject bitterly)* So you're faithful to your one love, eh? *(With an ugly smile, speaks nastily)* And how about her? Bet you she's out with a guy under some bush this minute, giving him all he wants.

RICHARD. *(Starting up in his chair—angrily)* Don't you say that! Don't you dare—!

BELLE. *(Unimpressed—with a cynical shrug of her shoulders, lightly and quickly)* All right. Have it your own way—and be a sucker! It cuts no ice with me.

RICHARD. You don't know her or—

BELLE *(Sharply)* And don't want to. Shut up about her, can't you? *(She stares before her bitterly.* RICHARD *subsides into scowling gloom.* RICHARD *turns away from* BELLE *and is facing* R., *leaning over his elbow on his knees and his head in his hands. He is becoming perceptibly more intoxicated with each moment now. The* BARTENDER *and the* SALESMAN *appear just inside* R. *door. The* BARTENDER *nods*

*toward* BELLE, *giving the* SALESMAN *a wink. The*
SALESMAN *grins and comes into the room, carrying
his highball in his hand. He is a stout, jowly-faced
man in his late thirties, dressed with cheap nattiness,
with the professional breeziness and jocular kid-'em-
along manner of his kind.* BELLE *looks up as he
enters and he and she exchange glance of complete
recognition. She knows his type by heart and he
knows hers.)*

SALESMAN. *(Crosses to table #1 at R., grinning
genially—sits in chair R. of table; speaks insinuatingly)* Good evening.

BELLE. *(Returning the smile and speaks with same
inflection)* Good evening.

SALESMAN. Hope I'm not butting in on your party
—but my dogs were giving out standing at that bar.

BELLE. *(Smiles at* SALESMAN) All right with me.
*(Giving* RICHARD *a rather contemptuous look, nods
her head toward him as she says)* I've got no party
on.

SALESMAN. *(Turns his chair to face them)* That
sounds hopeful.

RICHARD. *(Suddenly recites sentimentally)* "But
I wouldn't do such, 'cause I loved her too much, but
I learned about women from her." (RICHARD *raises
his head; looks with a scowl at the* SALESMAN, *seeing
him for the first time, then turns to* BELLE) Let's
have 'nother d.ink!

BELLE. You've had enough. (RICHARD *subsides,
muttering to himself—arm about* BELLE, *head on his
chest.)*

SALESMAN. What is it—a child poet or a child
actor?

BELLE. Don't know. Got me guessing.

SALESMAN. Well, if you could shake the cradle-
robbing act, maybe we could do a little business.

BELLE. That's easy. I just pull my freight. *(She
then shakes* RICHARD *by the arm; pushes his arms*

*away from her.* RICHARD *puts his arms about her
again.)* Listen, Kid. Here's an old friend of mine,
Mr. Smith of New Haven, just come in. (SALESMAN
*agrees; tips his hat but* BELLE *ignores him.)* I'm going
over and sit at his table for a while, see? And you
better go home.

RICHARD. *(Blinking at her and scowling)* I'm
never going home! I'll show them!

BELLE. *(Shrugging her shoulders—lightly)* Have
it your own way—only let me up. *(She takes his arm
from around her and goes to sit by the* SALESMAN.)

RICHARD. *(Stares after her offendedly)* Go on.
What do I care what you do? *(Drops his head on his
arms on table.)*

SALESMAN. *(As* BELLE *sits beside him)* Well,
what kind of beer will you have, Sister?

BELLE. Mine's a *gin rickey.*

SALESMAN. You've got extravagant tastes, I'm
sorry to see.

RICHARD. *(Suddenly begins to recite sepulchrally)*
"Yet each man kills the thing he loves,
  By each let this be heard."

SALESMAN. *(Grinning)* Say, this is rich! *(He
calls encouragement to* RICHARD) That's swell dope,
young feller. Give us some more.

RICHARD. *(Ignoring him—goes on more rhetoric-
ally)*
"Some do it with a bitter look,
  Some with a flattering word,
*(Rises; crosses a step toward them as he continues)*
  The coward does it with a kiss,
  The brave man with a sword!"
*(He stares at* BELLE *gloomily and mutters tragically.
Realizes he has to sit and sees chair* L. *of table* #2
*and crosses to it)* I did it with a kiss! I'm a coward.
*(Sits in chair* L. *of table* #2.)

SALESMAN. *(Lift)* That's the old stuff, Kid. You've

got something on the ball, all right, all right! **Give us another—right over the old pan, now!**

RICHARD. *(Rises, faces them and raises arm)* "Oho! They cried"—

BELLE. *(Turns on* RICHARD *and yells)* **Get the hook!**

RICHARD. *(Glowering at her—staggers to* L. *of table #1. Tragically)* "The world is wide,
But fettered limbs go lame!
And once, or twice, *(Business of throwing dice)*
To throw the dice
Is a gentlemanly game, *(Leans over table to* SALESMAN)
But he does not win who plays with Sin
In the Secret House of Shame!"

BELLE. *(Angrily)* Aw, can it! (RICHARD *goes up and sits in chair* L. *of table #2.)* Give us a rest from that bunk!

SALESMAN. *(Mockingly)* This gal of yours don't appreciate poetry. She's a lowbrow. But I'm the kid that eats it up. My middle name is Kelly and Sheets! Give us some more of the same!

BELLE. *(Surveying* RICHARD *contemptuously)* He's copped a fine skinful—and gee, he's hardly had anything.

RICHARD. *(Regards her bitterly—then suddenly starts to his feet bellicosely. Crosses to* L. *of table #1—to the* SALESMAN) I don't believe you ever knew this lady in New Haven at all! You just picked her up now! *(Crosses to* L. *of her)* You leave her alone, you hear! *(Puts a protecting arm about her)* You won't do anything to her—not while I'm here to protect her!

BELLE. *(Laughing, pushes* RICHARD L. *to* R. *of table #1)* Oh, my God! Listen to it!

SALESMAN. *(Overlap cue—rises; crosses down* C.) Ssshh! This is a scream! Wait! *(Crosses up to

RICHARD. *He addresses* RICHARD *in tone of exaggerted mock melodrama.* BELLE *stands* R. *of* SALESMAN.)
Curse you, Jack Dalton—*(Grabs* BELLE's *hand)*—if I won't unhand her, what then?

RICHARD. *(Threateningly)* I'll give you a good punch—punch—in the snoot, that's what! *(He starts toward* SALESMAN. BELLE *howls with laughter and sits in chair above table #1.)*

SALESMAN. *(With mock terror—screams in falsetto and dodges to down* R.) Help! Help! *(The* BARTENDER *comes in irritably, but he is used to this sort of thing and wants peace, which he now tries to get.)*

BARTENDER. Hey. Cut out the noise! What the hell's up with you?

SALESMAN. *(Laughing—winks at* BARTENDER) He's going to murder me.

RICHARD. *(Tipsily—has by now seated himself in chair* L. *of table #2)* He's too damn fresh.

SALESMAN. *(Then gets a bright idea for eliminating* RICHARD) Say, George! *(Seriously beckons to the* BARTENDER, *who crosses to him)* It's none of my business, Brother, but if I were in your boots I'd give this young souse the gate. He's under age; any fool can see that.

BARTENDER. *(Guiltily, crosses a step toward* RICHARD) He told me he was over eighteen.

SALESMAN. Yes, and I tell you I'm Teddy Roosevelt—but you don't have to believe me. If you're not looking for trouble, I'd advise you to get him started for some other gin mill and let them do the lying if anything comes up.

BARTENDER. Hmm. *(He turns to* RICHARD *and tries to get him to his feet)* Come on, now. On your way! You'll start no trouble in here! Beat it, now!

RICHARD. *(On his feet)* I will not beat it!

BARTENDER. Oho, won't you? *(He gives him a*

*shove toward* R. RICHARD *stumbles* R. *and bangs piano keys as he runs into piano.)*

BELLE. *(Callously)* Give him the bum's rush! I'm sick of his bull! *(RICHARD turns furiously and tries to punch the BARTENDER.)*

BARTENDER. *(Avoids the punch)* Oho, you would, would you! *(He grabs RICHARD by the back of the neck and the seat of the pants and marches him ignominiously toward the R. door.)*

RICHARD. Leggo of me, you dirty coward!

BARTENDER. Quiet now—or I'll pin a Mary Ann on your jaw that'll quiet you! *(He rushes him through the R. door and a moment later the outer DOORS are heard swinging back and forth.)*

SALESMAN. *(With a chuckle, crosses to chair L. of table #1)* Hand it to me, Kid! How was that for a slick way of getting rid of him?

BELLE. *(Suddenly sentimental)* Poor kid. I hope he makes home all right. I liked him—before he got soused.

SALESMAN. *(Standing L. of chair L. of table #1)* Who is he?

BELLE. The boy who's upstairs with my friend told me, but I didn't pay much attention. Name's Miller. His old man runs a paper in this one-horse burg, I think he said.

SALESMAN. *(Emits a whistle)* Phew! He must be Nat Miller's kid, then. *(WARN Curtain.)*

BARTENDER. *(Coming back from the bar—with a grin—crosses to table #3 and picks up glasses)* Well, he's on his way—with a good boot in the tail to help him!

SALESMAN. *(With a malicious chuckle. Lift— crosses toward BARTENDER a step or two)* Yes? Well, maybe that boot will cost you a job, Brother. Know Nat Miller who runs the *Globe?* That's his kid.

BARTENDER. *(His face falling)* The hell it is! Who said so?

SALESMAN. This baby doll. *(Crosses to down* R. *via below table #1)* Say, I'll go keep cases on him— see he gets on the trolley all right, anyway. Nat Miller's a good scout. *(He hurries out* R.*)*

BARTENDER. *(Viciously)* Damn the luck! If he ever finds out I served his kid, he'll run me out of town. *(He turns on* BELLE *furiously)* Why didn't you put me wise, you lousy tramp, you!

BELLE. Hey! I don't stand for that kind of talk— not from no hick beer-squirter like you, see!

BARTENDER. *(Furiously)* You don't, don't you! Who was it but you told me to hand him dynamite in that fizz? *(He gives her chair a push that almost throws her to the floor. Then crosses to door* L.C. *and opens it—then crosses to her again)* Beat it, you— and beat it quick—or I'll call Sullivan from the cor- ner and have you run in for street-walking! *(He gives her a push that lands her in family-entrance doorway* L.C.*)* Get the hell out of here—and no long waits!

BELLE. *(Turns in doorway and calls back viciously)* I'll fix you for this, you thick Mick, if I have to go to jail for it. *(She goes out and slams the door.)*

BARTENDER. *(Looks after her worriedly for a second—then shrugs his shoulders)* That's only her bull. *(Then with a sigh as he picks up glasses from table #3, wipes table top as he says)* Them lousy tramps is always getting this dump in Dutch!

## FAST CURTAIN

## ACT TWO

### SCENE II

*Same as Act One—sitting-room of the Miller home —about eleven o'clock the same night.*

MILLER *is sitting in his favorite rocking chair,
#4. He has discarded collar and tie, coat and
shoes, for comfort's sake, and wears an old,
worn, brown dressing-gown and disreputable-
looking carpet slippers. He has his reading specs
on and is running over items in a newspaper.
But his mind is plainly preoccupied and worried,
and he is not paying much attention to what he
reads.*

MRS. MILLER *sits in chair #1. She also has on
her specs. A sewing basket is on her lap and she
is trying hard to keep her attention fixed on the
doily she is doing. But, as in the case of her husband but much more apparently, her mind is preoccupied with another matter, and she is obviously on tenterhooks of nervous uneasiness.*

LILY *is sitting in the armchair #2. She is pretending to read a novel, but her attention wan-
ders, too, and her expression is sad, although
now it has lost all its bitterness and become sub-
missive and resigned again.*

MILDRED *sits at the desk at Left, writing two
words over and over again, stopping each time to
survey the result critically, biting her tongue,
intensely concentrated on her work.*

TOMMY *sits at the front end of the sofa at
Right. He has had a hard day and is terribly
sleepy but will not acknowledge it. His eyes blink
shut on him; his head begins to nod, but he isn't
giving up, and every time he senses any of the
family glancing in his direction, he goads himself into a bright-eyed wakefulness.*

MILDRED. *(Counts ten after Curtain, then finally
surveys the two words she has been writing critically
and is satisfied with them)* There! *(She takes the
paper over to her mother, crossing down stage of
table* R. *to* MRS. MILLER *and sits on arm of her chair)*

Look, Ma. I've been practising a new way of writing my name. Don't you think it's the real goods?

MRS. MILLER. *(Pulled out of her preoccupation—chidingly)* Don't talk that horrible slang. My goodness, if my mother'd ever heard me—

MILDRED. Well, don't you think it's nice, then?

MRS. MILLER. *(Sinks back into her preoccupation, then—scanning the paper with sightless eyes—vaguely)* Yes, very nice, Mildred—very nice, indeed. *(Hands the paper back mechanically.)*

MILDRED. *(Regards her mother's preoccupation and is a little piqued, but smiles)* Absent-minded! I don't believe you even saw it! *(Turns upstage without rising and shows it to* LILY. MILLER *gives an uneasy glance at his wife and then, as if afraid of meeting her eye, looks quickly back at his paper again.)*

MRS. MILLER. *(Staring before her—sighs worriedly)* Oh, I do wish that Richard would come home!

MILLER. *(Soothingly)* There now, Essie. He'll be in any minute now. Don't you worry about him.

MRS. MILLER. But I do worry about him! *(With another heavy sigh)* What time is it now, Nat? *(*MILDRED *puts arm about her mother's shoulder.)*

MILLER. *(Adopting a joking tone)* I'm going to buy a clock for in here. You have me reaching for my watch every couple of minutes. *(He has pulled his watch out of his vest pocket—with forced carelessness)* Only a little past ten.

MRS. MILLER. *(Indignantly)* Why, you said it was that an hour ago! Nat Miller, you're telling me a fib so's not to worry me. You let me see that watch!

MILLER. *(Guiltily)* Well, it's quarter to eleven—but that's not so late—when you remember it's the Fourth of July.

MRS. MILLER. *(Exasperatedly)* If you don't stop

talking Fourth of July—! (LILY *looks at* MRS. MIL-
LER, *then goes back to reading.*)

MILDRED. *(Has brought her paper around to her
father and now she shoves it under his nose. As she
leans against* L. *edge of table* R., *facing him. Lift)*
Look, Pa.

MILLER. *(Seizes on this interruption with eager
relief—scanning the paper)* Let's see. Hmm. Seems
to me you've been inventing a new signature each
week lately. What are you in training for—writing
checks? You must be planning to catch a rich husband.

MILDRED. *(With an arch toss of her head)* No
wedding bells for me! But how do you like it, Pa?

MILLER. It's overpowering—no other word for it,
overpowering! You could put it on the Declaration
of Independence and not feel ashamed! *(He passes
paper to* MILDRED. BOTH *laugh.)*

MRS. MILLER. *(Desolately, almost on the verge of
tears)* It's all right for you to laugh and joke with
Mildred! I'm the only one in this house seems to
care— *(Her lips tremble.)*

MILDRED. *(A bit disgustedly)* Ah, Ma, Dick only
sneaked off to the fireworks at the beach, you wait
and see.

MRS. MILLER. Those fireworks were over long ago.
If he had, he'd be home.

LILY. *(Soothingly)* He probably couldn't get a
seat, the trolleys are so jammed, and he had to walk
home.

MILLER. *(Seizing on this with relief)* Yes, I never
thought of that, but I'll bet that's it.

MILDRED. *(Rises, crosses to* L. *of* MRS. MILLER
*and sits on* L. *arm of her chair)* Ah, don't let him
worry you, Ma. He just wants to show off he's heartbroken about that silly Muriel—and get everyone
fussing over him and wondering if he hasn't drowned
himself or something.

MRS. MILLER. *(Snappily)* You be quiet! I really believe you're that hard-hearted you haven't got a heart in you! *(With an accusing glance at her husband—insinuatingly)* One thing I know, you don't get that from me! *(He chuckles and resumes reading paper. She sniffs and looks away from him around the room.)*

TOMMY. *(Who is nodding and blinking, is afraid her eye is on him. He straightens alertly and speaks in a voice that is, in spite of his effort, dripping with drowsiness. Speaks after MILLER starts to read again)* Let me see what you wrote, Mid.

MILDRED. *(Cruelly mocking)* You? You're so sleepy you couldn't see it!

TOMMY. *(Sits upright and then speaks valiantly)* I am not sleepy!

MRS. MILLER. *(Has fixed her eye on him)* My gracious, I was forgetting you were still up! You run up to bed this minute! It's hours past your bedtime!

TOMMY. *(Dolefully)* But it's the Fourth of July. Ain't it, Pa?

MRS. MILLER. *(Again gives her husband an accusing stare)* There! You see what you've done? You might know he'd copy your excuses! *(Then sharply, to TOMMY)* You heard what I said, Young Man!

TOMMY. *(Rising, crosses to her, touching her arm coaxingly)* Aw, Ma, can't I stay up a *little* longer?

MRS. MILLER. *(Lift)* I said no! You obey me and no more arguing about it!

TOMMY. Aw! I should think I could stay up till Dick—

MILLER. *(Kindly but firmly)* You heard your Ma say no more arguing. When she says git, you better git.

TOMMY. *(Accepts his fate resignedly and starts around kissing them all good night. Crosses to front of table* R., *leans over it and kisses* LILY) Good night, Aunt Lily.

LILY. *(Fondly)* Good night, dear. Sleep well.

TOMMY. *(Pecking at* MILDRED *but obviously not kissing her)* Good night, you.

MILDRED. Good night, you.

TOMMY. *(Sitting on arm of* MILLER'S *chair, snuggles against him)* Good night, Pa.

MILLER. Good night, Son. *(Kisses him)* Sleep tight. (TOMMY *continues to sit there until* MILLER *nudges him to go to bed.)*

TOMMY. *(Rises; crosses to* MRS. MILLER, *kissing her)* Good night, Ma.

MRS. MILLER. Good night. Here! You look feverish. *(She feels his brow with her left hand)* No, you're all right. Hurry up, now. And don't forget your prayers.

TOMMY. *(Goes slowly to the doorway* L.C. *via down stage to* L., *then turns suddenly when in doorway* L.C., *the discovery of another excuse lighting up his face. Crosses to above his father's chair and just* L. *of table* R.) Here's another thing, Ma. When I was up to the water closet last—

MRS. MILLER. *(Sharply)* When you were *where?*

TOMMY. The bathroom.

MRS. MILLER. That's better.

TOMMY. *(Sits in chair #3)* Uncle Sid was snoring like a fog horn—and he's right next to my room. How can I ever get to sleep while he's— *(He is overcome by a jaw-cracking yawn.)*

MRS. MILLER. I guess you'd get to sleep all right if you were inside a fog horn! You run along now! (TOMMY *gives up, grins sleepily and moves off to bed. Exits* L.C. *As soon as he is off her mind, all her former uneasiness comes back on* MRS. MILLER *tenfold. She sighs, moves restlessly, then finally asks)* What time is it now, Nat?

MILLER. Now, Essie, I just told you a minute ago.

Mrs. Miller. *(Resentfully)* I don't see how you can take it so calm! Here it's midnight, you might say— (Arthur *starts to walk back stage as though he had come up the stairs of the porch that runs all the way around the house and was now walking around to the front door.)* —and our Richard still out, and we don't even know where he is.

Mildred. There's someone! *(Runs to doorway* L.C.*)* Bet that's him now, Ma.

Mrs. Miller. *(Her anxiety immediately turning to relieved anger)* You give him a good piece of your mind, Nat! You're too easy with him, that's the whole trouble! (Someone *whistling "March, March Down the Field." Yale Song.)*

Mildred. *(Gets chair from down* L.C., *brings it to* L. *of* Miller *and sits)* No, that isn't Dick. It's Art.

Mrs. Miller. *(Her face falling)* Oh! *(A moment later* Arthur *enters* L.C., *whistling softly half under his breath, looking complacently pleased with himself. Crosses to upper* L. *end of table* R.*)*

Miller. *(Surveys him over his glasses, not with enthusiasm—shortly)* So you're back, eh? We thought it was Richard.

Arthur. *(Standing* R. *end above of* Miller*)* Is he still out? Where'd he go to?

Miller. That's just what we'd like to know. You didn't run into him anywhere, did you?

Arthur. No. I've been at the Rands' ever since dinner. *(Takes out pipe and pouch and begins to fill pipe)* I suppose he sneaked off to the beach to watch the fireworks.

Miller. *(Pretending an assurance he is far from feeling)* Of course. That's what we've been trying to tell your mother, but she insists on worrying her head off.

Mrs. Miller. But if he was going to the fireworks, why wouldn't he say so? He knew we'd let him.

Arthur. *(With calm wisdom)* That's easy, Ma.

*(He grins superiorly)* Didn't you hear him this morning showing off bawling out the Fourth like an anarchist? He wouldn't want to reneg on that to you—but he'd want to see the old fireworks just the same. *(He adds complacently)* I know. He's at the foolish age. *(Sits chair #3.)*

MILLER. *(Stares at* ARTHUR *with ill-concealed astonishment, then grins, jokingly)* Well, Arthur, by gosh, you make me feel as if I owed you an apology when you talk horse sense like that! *(He turns to his wife, greatly relieved)* Arthur's hit the nail right on the head, I think, Essie. That's where he is—

MRS. MILLER. *(With a sigh of relief)* Well— *(Worried again)* I wish he was home.

ARTHUR. *(Lights pipe with solemn gravity)* He oughtn't to be allowed out this late at his age. I wasn't—Fourth or no Fourth—if I remember.

MILLER. *(A twinkle in his eyes)* Don't tax your memory trying to recall those ancient days of your youth. (MILDRED *laughs and* ARTHUR *looks sheepish. But he soon regains his aplomb and changes the subject tactfully.)*

ARTHUR. *(Importantly)* We had a corking dinner at the Rands'. We had sweetbreads on toast.

MRS. MILLER. *(Arising momentarily from her depression)* Just like the Rands to put on airs before you! I never could see anything to sweetbreads. Always taste like soap to me. And no real nourishment to them. I wouldn't have the pesky things on my table! (ARTHUR *again feels sat upon.)*

MILDRED. *(Teasingly)* Did you kiss Elsie good night?

ARTHUR. *(Gruffly)* Stop trying to be so darn funny all the time! *(Lift—leans over* MILLER *toward* MILDRED) You give me a pain in the ear!

MILDRED. *(Huffily, leans over* MILLER *toward* ARTHUR) And that's where she gives me a pain, the stuck-up thing! Thinks she's the whole cheese!

MILLER. *(Irritably, caught between them)* And it's where your everlasting wrangling gives me a pain, you two. Give us a rest! *(MILDRED rises, returns to desk, writing her name. There is silence for a moment.)*

MRS. MILLER. *(Suddenly sighs worriedly again)* I do wish that boy would get home!

*(WARN Light.)*

MILLER. *(Glances at her uneasily, peeks surreptitiously at his watch—then has an inspiration and turns to ARTHUR)* Arthur, what's this I hear about your having such a good singing voice? Rand was telling me he liked nothing better than to hear you sing— said you did every night you were up there. Why don't you ever give us folks at home here a treat? Why not give us a song or two now? You can play for him, can't you, Mildred?

MILDRED. *(With a toss of her head)* I can play as well as Elsie Rand, at least!

ARTHUR. *(Ignoring her—clearing his throat importantly)* I've been singing a lot tonight, Pa. I don't know if my voice—

MILDRED. *(Forgetting her grudge, rises and runs to ARTHUR. Grabs her brother's hand and tugs at it)* Come on. Don't play modest. You know you're just dying to show off! *(This puts ARTHUR off it at once. He snatches his hand away from her angrily. MILDRED is now standing up R.C.)*

ARTHUR. Let go of me, you! *(Then with surly dignity)* I don't feel like singing tonight, Pa. I will some other time.

MILLER. *(Sharply)* You let him alone, Mildred! *(Then he winks at ARTHUR, indicating with his eyes and a nod of head MRS. MILLER, who has again sunk into worried brooding. He makes it plain by this pantomime that he wants him to sing to distract his mother's mind.)*

ARTHUR. *(Puts aside his pipe and gets up prompt-*

*ly. Lift)* Oh—sure, I'll do the best I can. *(He follows* MILDRED *off* L.C., *where he switches on the* LIGHTS.)          *(Music cue. SCALE.)   (LIGHTS.)*

MILLER. *(To his wife—reassuringly)* It won't keep Tommy awake. Nothing could. *(SCALE.)* And Sid, he'd sleep through an earthquake. *(Then suddenly, looking through the front parlor—grumpily)* Darn it, speak of the devil, here he comes. Well, he's had a good sleep and he'd ought to be sobered up. (LILY *gets up from her chair and looks around her huntedly, as if for a place to hide.* MILLER *says soothingly)* Lily, you just sit down and read your book and don't pay any attention to him.

*(MUSIC Stops.)*

*(She sits down again and bends over her book tensely. From the front parlor comes the tinkling of a PIANO as* MILDRED *runs over the scales. In the midst of this,* SID *enters* L.C. *All the effervescence of his jag has worn off and he is now suffering from a bad case of hangover—nervous, sick, a prey to gloomy remorse and bitter feelings of self-loathing and self-pity. His eyes are bloodshot and puffed, his baldness tousled and tufty. He sidles into the room guiltily, his eyes shifting about, avoiding looking at anyone.)*

SID. *(Blurts out, forcing a sickly twitching smile after he is seated)* Hello.

MILLER. *(Considerately casual)* Hello, Sid. Had a good nap?

SID. *(Miserably self-conscious and ill-at-ease. After swallowing hard, suddenly blurts out)* Essie, Nat and—and Lily— I—I want to apologize—for coming home—the way I did—there's no excuse—but I didn't mean—

MILLER. *(Sympathetically)* Of course, Sid. It's all forgotten.

MRS. MILLER. *(Rousing herself—affectionately pitying)* Don't be a goose, Sid. We know how it is with picnics. You forget it. (MILDRED *begins to play the introduction of "Dearie."*)

*(Music cue "Dearie.")*

MILDRED. Try this one.

ARTHUR. All right. (ARTHUR *begins to sing. He has a fairly decent voice but his method is untrained sentimentality to a dripping degree. He sings that old sentimental favorite "Dearie." The effect on his audience is instant.* MILLER *gazes before him with a ruminating melancholy, his face seeming to become gently sorrowful and old.* MRS. MILLER *stares before her, her expression becoming more and more doleful.* LILY *tries to read.* SID *is moved to his remorseful, guilt-stricken depths.* SID's *face lights up a bit but his gaze shifts to* LILY *with a mute appeal, hoping for a word from her which is not forthcoming. Her eyes are fixed on her book, her body tense and rigid.)*

SID. *(Finally blurts out desperately)* Lily—I'm sorry—about the fireworks. Can you—forgive me? *(But* LILY *remains implacably silent. A stricken look comes over* SID's *face.)*

MILLER. *(Comes to* SID's *rescue)* Ssshh! Arthur's going to sing for us. Sit down, Sid. (SID, *hanging his head, flees to the farthest corner, L., front, and sits, facing front, hunched up, elbows on knees, face in hands. His round eyes, childishly wounded and woe-begone.* ARTHUR *sings "Dearie, my Dearie, nothing's worth while but dreams of you—" etc.— playing up its sentimental values for all he is worth. The effect on his audience is that of the previous song, intensified—especially upon* SID. LILY *tries to read her book but looks over it, her face growing tragically sad. As he finishes,* MILLER *again starts and applauds)* Mighty fine, Arthur! You sang that darned well. (KIDS *laugh.)* Didn't he, Essie?

MRS. MILLER. *(Dolefully)* Yes—but I wish **he**

wouldn't sing such sad songs. *(Then, her lips trembling)* Richard's always whistling that.

MILLER. *(Hastily calls)* Give us something cheery, next one, Arthur— You know, just for variety's sake—

ARTHUR. *(Off stage)* All right, Pa.

SID. *(Suddenly turns toward* LILY—*his voice husky and choked with tears—in a passion of self-denunciation)* You're right, Lily!—right not to forgive me! I'm no good and never will be! You shouldn't even wipe your feet on me!—no good to myself or anybody else! If I had any guts I'd kill myself, and good riddance!—but I haven't! I'm yellow, too!—a yellow, drunken bum! *(He hides his face in his hands and begins to sob like a sick little boy. This is too much for* LILY. *All her bitter hurt and steely resolve to ignore and punish him vanish in a flash, swamped by a pitying love for him. She runs and puts her arm around him—even kisses him tenderly and impulsively on his bald head, and soothes him as if he were a little boy.* MRS. MILLER, *almost equally moved, has half risen to go to her brother, too, but* MILLER *winks and shakes his head vigorously and motions her to sit down.)*

LILY. *(Rises and crosses to him)* There! Don't cry, Sid! I can't bear it! Of course I forgive you. Haven't I always forgiven you? I know you're not to blame—so don't, Sid!

SID. *(Lifts a tearful, humbly grateful, pathetic face to her—but a face that the dawn of a cleansed conscience is already beginning to restore to its natural Puckish expression)* Do you really forgive me— I know I don't deserve it— Can you really—?

LILY. *(Gently)* I told you I did, Sid—and I do. *(*MILDRED *plays "Waiting at the Church," starting with chorus and no introduction.)*

SID. *(Kisses her hand humbly, like a big puppy.*

*licking it)* Thanks, Lily. I can't tell you— *(In the front parlor,* ARTHUR *begins to sing rollickingly, "Waiting at the Church," and after the first line or two* MILDRED *joins in.* SID'S *face lights up with appreciation and, automatically, he begins to tap one foot in time, still holding fast to* LILY'S *hand. When they come to "sent around a note, this is what he wrote," he can no longer resist, but joins in a shaky bawl)* "Can't get away to marry you today. My wife won't let me!" *(As the song finishes, the* TWO *in the other room laugh.* MILLER *and* SID *laugh.* LILY *smiles at* SID'S *laughter. Only* MRS. MILLER *remains dolefully preoccupied, as if she hadn't heard.)*

MILLER. That's fine, Arthur and Mildred. That's darned good.

ARTHUR. *(Off stage)* Thanks, Pa.

SID. *(Turning to* LILY *enthusiastically)* You ought to hear Vesta Victoria sing that! Gosh, she's great! I heard her at Hammerstein's Victoria— You remember, that trip I made to New York.

LILY. *(Her face suddenly grown tired and sad again—for her memory of certain aspects of that trip is the opposite from what he would like to recall at this moment—gently disengaging her hand from his—with a hopeless sigh. Crosses to chair #2, end of table, then speaks)* Yes, I remember, Sid. *(Sits. He is overcome momentarily by guilty confusion. She goes quietly and sits in chair #2. In the front parlor,* MILDRED *plays "I Can't Make My Eyes Behave" rather quietly. She and* ARTHUR *whistle it softly.)*

MRS. MILLER. *(After a slight pause. Suddenly —in a worried tone)* What time is it now, Nat? *(Then, without giving him a chance to answer)* Oh, I'm getting worried something dreadful. Nat! You don't know what might have happened to Richard! You read in the papers every day about boys getting run over by automobiles.

LILY. *(Frightenedly)* Oh, don't say that, Essie!

MILLER. *(Sharply, to conceal his own reawakened apprehension)* Don't get to imagining things, now!

MRS. MILLER. Well, why couldn't it happen, with everyone that owns one out tonight, and lots of those driving drunk? *(On the verge of hysteria)* Oh, I know something dreadful's happened! And you can sit there listening to songs and laughing as if— Why don't you do something? *(MUSIC stops abruptly.)* Why don't you go out and find him? *(She bursts into tears.)*

LILY. *(Comes to her quickly and puts her arm around her)* Essie, you mustn't worry so! You'll make yourself sick!

MILDRED. *(Comes hurrying in from L.C. Runs to R. of MRS. MILLER and sits arm of her chair)* What's the trouble? *(ARTHUR appears in the doorway beside her.)* Ah, don't cry, Ma! Dick'll turn up in a minute or two, wait and see!

ARTHUR. *(Crowds in L. of LILY)* Sure, he will.

MILLER. *(Gets to his feet, frowning—soberly)* I was going out to look—if he wasn't back by twelve sharp. But I'll go now, if it'll ease your mind. I'll take the auto and drive out the beach road— *(He has crossed to up L.C. by this time and is unconsciously starting to get his bathrobe off)* You better come with me, Arthur.

ARTHUR. *(Lift)* Sure thing, Pa. *(Suddenly he listens and says)* Shhh! That must be him now.

*(NOISE for RICHARD's entrance.)*

MRS. MILLER. *(Overlap Cue)* Oh, thank God!

MILLER. *(With a sheepish smile)* Darn him! I'll give him hell for worrying us all like this! *(Crosses to down extreme R. Then RICHARD lurches in violently L.C. Door is open. He slides to R. of desk chair and leans against it, facing the OTHERS. He is trying for dignity, and his eyes are glassed and wild. He leans with back against desk chair. The knees of his trou-*

*sers are dirty, one of them torn from the sprawl on the sidewalk he had taken, following the* BARTENDER'S *kick. They* ALL *gape at him, too paralyzed for a moment to say anything.* SID *rises; crosses to* L. *of* ARTHUR.)                          *(WARN Curtain.)*

MRS. MILLER.  Richard! Oh, God, what's happened to him! He's gone crazy!

SID.  *(The first to regain presence of mind—overlap cue)* Crazy, nothing. He's only soused!

RICHARD.  *(With a wild gesture of defiance, maudlingly dramatic. Staggers to chair #4 and flops into it)*
    "Yesterday this Day's Madness did prepare
    Tomorrow's Silence, Triumph, or Despair.
    Drink! for—"

MILLER.  *(His face grown stern and angry, takes a threatening step toward him)* Richard! How—!

MRS. MILLER.  *(Hysterically)* Don't you strike him, Nat! Don't you—

SID.  *(Grabbing his arm)* Steady, Nat! The boy don't know what he's doing!

RICHARD.  *(Drunkenly glorying in the sensation he is creating—recites with heroic, dramatic emphasis)* "And then—at ten o'clock—Eilert Lovborg will come—with vine leaves in my hair!" *(He laughs dramatically with a double-eyed sardonicism.)*

MRS. MILLER.  *(Staring at him as if she couldn't believe her eyes)* Richard! You're intoxicated—! You bad, wicked boy, you!

RICHARD.  *(Forces a wicked leer to his lips and quotes with ponderous mockery)* "Fancy that, Hedda!" *(Then suddenly his whole expression changes. His pallor takes on a greenish, sea-sick tinge, his eyes seem to be turned inward uneasily—he realizes he is home—looks about—sees his mother.)*

MRS. MILLER.  Do you hear him talking about some Hedda? He's been with one of those bad women.

RICHARD.  *(All pose gone, he calls to his mother*

*appealingly, like a sick little boy)* Ma! (MRS. MILLER
*rises, dropping sewing on floor.)* I feel—rotten!
*(Sits chair #4—at no time does he make any gesture
to indicate nausea.* MRS. MILLER *gives a cry and
starts to go to him, but* SID *interrupts her.)*

SID. Wait a minute, Essie. *(Persuasively—starts
to help* RICHARD *out of chair)* You let me take care
of him, Essie. I know this game backwards. *(Has
him to his feet and they are clearing the chairs to go
up* L. *as the*

## CURTAIN FALLS

# ACT THREE

## Scene I

SCENE: *The same—Sitting-room of the Miller home —about one in the afternoon of the following day.*

AT RISE: *As the Curtain rises the family are all waiting and watching* MILLER. NAT MILLER *is standing down Left looking out window, smoking the end of a good cigar. There is quite a pause before he speaks. He looks at them, then speaks. His face is set in an expression of frowning severity.* MRS. MILLER *is sitting in armchair #1. Her face is drawn and worried. She has evidently had no rest yet from a long, sleepless, tearful night.* SID *is seated in armchair #2. He is himself again, his expression as innocent as if nothing had occurred the previous day to remotely concern him. And outside of eyes that are bloodshot and nerves that are shaky, he shows no after-effects except that he is terribly sleepy.* LILY *is seated on upper end of sofa, Right. She is gently sad and depressed.* MILDRED *is seated Right of* LILY *on sofa, Left of* ARTHUR. *She is subdued and covertly watching her father.* ARTHUR *is seated Right of* MILDRED *and Left of* TOMMY *on sofa. He is self-consciously a virtuous young man against whom nothing can be said.* TOMMY *is seated on down*

93

*stage end of sofa. He is Right of* ARTHUR. *He is subdued and covertly watches his father. The atmosphere is as stiltedly grave as if they were attending a funeral service. Their eyes keep fixed on the head of the house, who has gone to the window at Left and is staring out frowningly, savagely chewing a toothpick.* SID *glances at* MRS. MILLER. MRS. MILLER *at* MILLER.

MILLER. *(Finally—pause—counts five; crosses up* L. *a step.* SID *looks at* MILLER. *Irritably)* Damn it, I'd ought to be back at the office putting in some good licks! *(Starts up* L.*)* I've a whole pile of things that have got to be done today!

MRS. MILLER. *(Accusingly)* You don't mean to tell me you're going back without seeing him!

MILLER. *(Exasperatedly. Stops* R. *of armchair* L.C.*)* 'Course I'm not! I wish you'd stop jumping to conclusions! *(Puts cigar butt on tray on table* R.*)* What else did I come home for, I'd like to know? *(He ends up very lamely and is irritably conscious of the fact and starts to cross up* L. ARTHUR *looks at* LILY. SID *glances at* LILY, *then front. Then* TOMMY *speaks.)*

TOMMY. *(Who has been fidgetting restlessly—unable to bear the suspense a moment longer. Loudly)* What's Dick done? Why is everyone scared to tell me?

MILLER. *(Seizes this as an escape valve—turns and fixes his youngest son with a stern, forbidding eye. Crosses to* TOMMY*)* Young man, I've never spanked you yet, but that don't mean I never will! You keep your mouth shut till you're spoken to—or I warn you something's going to happen! *(Crosses to below table.)*

MRS. MILLER. Yes, Tommy, you keep still and don't bother your Pa. *(Then warningly to her hus-*

*band, just after he has crossed to her)* Careful what you say, Nat. Little pitchers have big ears.

MILLER. *(Peremptorily. L.C.—faces them)* You kids skedaddle—all of you. (TOMMY *and* MILDRED *rise and exit up* L.) Why are you always hanging around the house? Go out and play in the yard, or take a walk and get some fresh air! (MILDRED *takes* TOMMY'S *hands and leads him out up* L. ARTHUR *hangs back as if the designation "kids" couldn't possibly apply to him. His father notices this—impatiently)* Arthur! (ARTHUR *goes out with a stiff, wounded dignity up* L.)

LILY. *(Tactfully)* I think I'll go for a walk, too. *(She goes out through* L.C. SID *makes a movement as if to follow her.)*

MILLER. I'd like you to stay, Sid—for a while, anyway. *(Crosses to lower end of sofa* R. *via below table as he continues)* Where is Richard?

MRS. MILLER. *(Flusteredly)* He's still in bed. I made him stay in bed to punish him—and I thought he ought to, anyway, after being so sick. But he says he feels all right.

SID. *(With another yawn)* 'Course he does. When you're young you can stand anything without it fazing you. Why, I remember when I could come down on the morning after fresh as a daisy and eat a breakfast of pork chops and fried onions and— *(He stops guiltily and very shortly falls asleep.)*

MILLER. *(Bitingly)* I suppose that was before eating lobsters shells had ruined your iron constitution!

MRS. MILLER. *(Regards her brother severely)* If I was in your shoes, I'd keep still! *(Then, turning to* MILLER) Richard *must* be feeling *better.* He ate all the dinner I sent up, Norah says.

MILLER. *(Accusingly)* I thought you weren't going to give him any dinner—to punish him.

MRS. MILLER. *(Guiltily)* Well—in his weakened

condition—I thought it best— *(Then defensively)*
But you needn't think I haven't punished him. I've
given him pieces of my mind he won't forget in a
hurry. And I've kept reminding him his real punishment was still to come—that you were coming home
to dinner on purpose—and then he'd learn that you
could be terrible stern when he did such awful things.

MILLER. *(Stirs uncomfortably, rises and crosses
to down C.)* Hmm!

MRS. MILLER. And that's just what it's your duty
to do—punish him good and hard! *(Then hastily)*
But you be careful how you go about it, Nat. (MIL-
LER *stops and glances at her—then to up* C. *and up* R.)
Remember he's like you inside—too sensitive for his
own good. *(Front)* And he never would have done
it, I know, if it hadn't been for that darned little
dunce—(MILLER *continues cross to lower end of
sofa.)*—Muriel, and her numbskull father—and then
all of us teasing him and hurting his feelings all day
—*(To* MILLER*)*—and then you lost your temper and
were so sharp with him right after dinner before he
went out.

MILLER. *(Resentfully, looking at her. Reaches
down* R. *in time for line and sits after cue and then
speaks)* I see this is going to work round to where
it's all my fault!

MRS. MILLER. Now, I didn't say that— *(To* SID)
Did I? *(Sees* SID *is now comfortably asleep)* And
here's another thing. You know as well as I, Richard
would never have done such a thing alone. Why, he
wouldn't know how! He must have been influenced
and led by someone!

MILLER. Yes, I believe that. Did you worm out
of him who it was? *(Then angrily)* By God, I'll
make whoever it was regret it!

MRS. MILLER. No, he wouldn't admit there was
any one. *(Then triumphantly. Rises; crosses to sofa;
sits above* MILLER) But there is one thing I did

worm out of him—and I can tell you it relieved my
mind more'n anything! You know, I was afraid he'd
been with one of those bad women. Well, turns out
there wasn't any Hedda. She was just out of those
books he's been reading. *(Then lamely)* So some-
how—I can't kind of feel it's all as bad as I thought
it was. *(Then quickly and indignantly)* But it's bad
enough, goodness knows— The idea of a boy of his
age! Shall I go up now and tell him to get dressed,
you want to see him? *(Rises and crosses up L.)*

MILLER. *(A bit helplessly—and irritably. Crosses
to down C. and to up L.C.)* Yes! I can't waste all day
listening to you—

MRS. MILLER. *(Worriedly. In door L.C.)* Now
you keep your temper, Nat, remember! *(She goes
out.)*

MILLER. Darn women, anyway! They always get
you mixed up. Their minds simply don't know what
logic is! *(Then he notices that SID is dozing, his
head nodding. Sharply. Crosses to L. and rear of
SID)* Sid! Sid! *(Nudges SID.)*

SID. *(Blinking—mechanically, but very quietly)*
I'll take the same. *(Then hurriedly)* What'd you say,
Nat?

MILLER. *(Caustically)* What I didn't say was
"what'll you have." *(Then irritably)* Do you want
to be of some help, or don't you? *(SID nods.)* Then
keep awake and try and use your brains! This is a
damned sight more serious than Essie has any idea!
She thinks there weren't any girls mixed up with
Richard's spree last night—but I happen to know
there were! *(He takes a letter from his pocket)*
Here's a note a woman left with one of the boys
downstairs at the office this morning—didn't ask to
see me, just said give me this. He'd never seen her
before—said she looked like a tart. *(He has opened
the letter and reads)* "Your son got the booze he
drank last night at the Pleasant Beach House. The

bartender there knew he was under age but served him just the same. He thought it was a good joke to get him soused. If you have any guts you will run that bastard out of town." Well, what do you think of that? It's a woman's handwriting—not signed, of course.

SID. She's one of the babies, all right—judging from her elegant language.

MILLER. *(Handing him the letter)* See if you recognize the handwriting.

SID. *(With a reproachful look)* Nat, I resent the implication that I correspond with all the tramps around this town. *(Then, looking at the letter)* No, *I don't know* who *this* could be. *(Handing the letter back)* But I deduce that the lady had a run-in with the barkeep and wants revenge.

MILLER. *(Grimly)* And I deduce that before that she must have picked up Richard—or how would she know who he was?—and took him to this dive.

SID. Maybe. The Pleasant Beach House is nothing but a bed house— *(Quickly)* At least, so I've been told. I hope you're wrong, Nat. That kind of baby is dangerous for a kid like Dick—in more ways than one. You know what I mean.

MILLER. *(Frowningly)* Yep—and that's just what's got me worried. *(Sits chair #3)* Damn it, I've got to have a straight talk with him—about women and all those things. I ought to have long ago.

SID. Yes. You ought.

MILLER. I've tried to a couple of times—but, hell, I always get sort of ashamed of myself and can't get started right. You feel, in spite of all his bold talk out of books, that he's so darned innocent inside.

SID. I know. I wouldn't like the job. *(Then after a pause—curiously)* How were you figuring to punish him for his sins?

MILLER. *(Frowning)* To be honest with you, Sid, I'm damned if I know. It all depends on what I feel about what he feels when I first size him up—and even then it'll be like shooting in the dark.

SID. *(After a pause)* If I didn't know you so well, I'd say don't be too hard on him. *(He smiles a little bitterly)* If you remember, I was always getting punished—and see what a lot of good it did me!

MILLER. *(Kindly)* Oh, there's lots worse than you around, so don't take to boasting. *(Then at a sound from the front parlor—with a sigh. MRS. MILLER'S footsteps)* Well, here comes the bad man, I guess.

SID. *(Getting up)* I'll beat it. *(But it is MRS. MILLER who appears L.C., looking guilty and defensive. SID sits down again in chair #2.)*

MRS. MILLER. *(In doorway L.C.)* I'm sorry, Nat—but he was sound asleep (MILLER *"Hum"*) and I didn't have the heart to wake him.

MILLER. *(Concealing a relief of which he is ashamed—exasperatedly)* Well, I'll be double damned! If you're not the—

MRS. MILLER. *(Defensively aggressive; crosses to L. of MILLER)* Now don't lose your temper at me, Nat Miller! You know as well as I do he needs all the sleep he can get today—after last night's ructions! Do you want him to be taken down sick? *(Crosses to chair L.C.)* You can see him when you come home for supper, can't you? My goodness, you'd think you couldn't bear waiting to punish him! *(Sits chair L.C.)*

MILLER. *(Outraged)* Well, I'll be eternally— *(Then suddenly he laughs)* No use talking, you certainly take the cake! But you know darned well I told you I'm not coming home to supper tonight. I've got a date with Jack Lawson that may mean a lot of new advertising and it's important.

MRS. MILLER. Then you can see him when you do come home.

MILLER. *(Covering his evident relief at this respite with a fuming manner. Rises)* All right! All right!

I give up! I'm going back to the office. *(He starts for the front parlor)* Bring a man all the way back here on a busy day and then you— No consideration— *(He disappears, and a moment later the front DOOR is heard shutting behind him.)*

MRS. MILLER. *(Crosses to* SID*)* Well! I never saw Nat so bad-tempered!

SID. *(With a chuckle)* He's so tickled to get out of it for a while he can't see straight!

MRS. MILLER. *(With a sniff)* I hope I know him better than you. *(Then fussing about the room, setting this and that in place, while* SID *yawns drowsily and blinks his eyes)* And there was Richard sleeping like a baby—so innocent-looking! *(Crosses to desk)* You'd think butter wouldn't melt in his mouth! It all goes to show you never can tell by appearances— not even when it's your own child. The idea!

SID. *(Drowsily)* Oh, Dick's all right, Essie. Stop worrying.

MRS. MILLER. *(With a sniff. Still facing desk)* Of course, you'd say that. I suppose you'll have him out with you painting the town red the next thing! *(As she is talking,* RICHARD *appears in the doorway* L.C. *He shows no ill effects from his experience the night before. In fact, he looks surprisingly healthy. He is dressed in flannel undershirt, trousers, shoes, covered by heavy brown bathrobe. His expression is one of hang-dog guilt mingled with defensive defiance.)*

RICHARD. *(With self-conscious unconcern, ignoring his mother; crosses down stage to lower end of sofa—and sits. He looks at* SID, *who looks at him. They both start to grin.* RICHARD *grins sheepishly and looks away from* SID *as he says)* Hello, Uncle Sid.

MRS. MILLER. *(Whirls on him; crosses to him)* What are you doing here, young man? I thought you were asleep! Seems to me you woke up pretty quick —just after your Pa left the house!

RICHARD. *(Sulkily)* I wasn't asleep.

MRS. MILLER. *(Outraged)* Do you mean to say you were deliberately deceiving?

RICHARD. I wasn't deceiving— You didn't ask if I was asleep.

MRS. MILLER. And imagine me standing there, and feeling sorry for you, like a fool— But you wait till your Pa comes back tonight. If you don't catch it—

RICHARD. *(Sulkily)* I don't care.

MRS. MILLER. You don't care? You talk as if you weren't sorry for what you did last night!

RICHARD. *(Defiantly)* I'm not sorry.

MRS. MILLER. Richard.

RICHARD. *(With bitter despondency)* I'm not sorry because I don't care a darn what I did, or anything about anything! But I won't do it again—

MRS. MILLER. *(Seizing on this to relent a bit)* Well, I'm glad to hear you say that, anyway!

RICHARD. But that's not because I think it was wicked or any such old-fogey *moral* notion, but because it wasn't any fun. It didn't make me happy and funny like it does Uncle Sid—

SID. *(Who has been dozing—drowsily)* What's that? Who's funny?

RICHARD. *(Ignoring him)* It only made me sadder —and sick—so I don't see any sense in it.

MRS. MILLER. Now you're talking sense! That's a good boy.

RICHARD. But I'm not sorry I tried it *once*— "curing the soul by means of the senses," as Oscar Wilde says.

MRS. MILLER. *(Then solicitously, putting her hand on head)* How's your headache? Do you want me to get you some Bromo Seltzer?

RICHARD. *(Taken down—disgustedly—rises and crosses to armchair #1 and sits)* No, I don't! Aw, Ma, you don't understand anything!

MRS. MILLER. *(Practically)* Well, I understand this much: It's your liver, that's what! You'll take a good dose of salts tomorrow morning, and no nonsense about it! *(Then suddenly)* My goodness, I wonder what time it's getting to be. I've got to go upstreet. *(She goes to the doorway L.C. as she speaks. RICHARD pays no attention to this.)* You stay here, Richard, you hear? Remember you're not allowed out today—for a punishment. *(She hurries away. RICHARD is sitting in tragic gloom. SID, without opening his eyes, speaks to him drowsily)*

SID. Well, how's my fellow Rum Pot? Got a head?

RICHARD. *(Startled—a bit sheepishly)* Aw, don't go dragging that up, Uncle Sid. *(Seriously)* I'm never going to be such a *fool* again, I tell you.

SID. *(With drowsy cynicism—not unmixed with bitterness at the end—absolutely no self pity)* Never again, eh? Seems to me I've heard someone say that before.

RICHARD. *(Darkly)* I was desperate, Uncle—even if she wasn't worth it. I was wounded to the heart.

SID. I like "to the quick" better myself—more stylish! *(Then sadly and bitterly—as he uncrosses his legs)* But you're right. Love is hell on a poor sucker. *(Touches RICHARD's arm)* Don't I know it? (SID's *chin sinks on his chest and he begins to breathe noisily, fast asleep. There is a sound of someone on the porch and the screen door is opened and MILDRED enters up L. She smiles on seeing her uncle, then gives a start on seeing RICHARD.)*

MILDRED. *(Crossing to down L.C.)* Hello! Are you allowed up?

RICHARD. Of course, I'm allowed up.

MILDRED. *(Crosses to sofa via below table R.)* How did Pa punish you?

RICHARD. He didn't. He went back to the office without seeing me.

MILDRED. Well, you'll catch it later. *(Then rebukingly. Sits on sofa)* And you ought to. If you'd ever seen how awful you looked last night!

RICHARD. *(Stirs uncomfortably)* Aw, forget it, can't you?

MILDRED. Well, are you ever going to do it again, that's what I want to know.

RICHARD. What's that to you?

MILDRED. *(With suppressed excitement)* Well, if you don't solemnly swear you won't—then I won't give you something I've got for you.

RICHARD. Don't try to kid me. You haven't got anything.

MILDRED. I have, too.

RICHARD. What?

MILDRED. Wouldn't you like to know! I'll give you three guesses.

RICHARD. *(Sits upright and says warningly)* Don't bother me. I'm in no mood to play riddles with kids! *(Sinks back into chair again.)*

MILDRED. Oh, well, if you're going to get snippy! Anyway, you haven't promised yet.

RICHARD. *(A prey to keen curiosity now)* I promise. What is it?

MILDRED. What would you like best in the world?

RICHARD. *(Trying to control curiosity)* I don't know. What?

MILDRED. And you pretend to be in love! If I told Muriel that!

RICHARD. *(Breathlessly)* Is it—from her? *(Turning chair toward MILDRED.)*

MILDRED. *(Laughing. Tempo)* Well, I guess it's a shame to keep you guessing. Yes. It is from her. I was walking past her place just now when I saw her waving from their parlor window, and I went up and she said "give this to Dick," and she didn't have a chance to say anything else because her mother called her and said she wasn't allowed to have company. So I took it—and here it is. *(She gives him a letter folded many times into a tiny square. RICHARD opens it with a trembling eagerness and reads. MIL-*

DRED *watches him curiously.* RICHARD *then sighs affectedly.)* Gee, it must be wonderful to be in love like you are—

RICHARD. *(His eyes shining with joy)* Gee, Mid, do you know what she says—that she didn't mean a word in that other letter. Her old man made her write it. And she loves me and only me and always will, no matter how they punish her!

MILDRED. *(A bit superior)* My! I'd never think *she* had that much *spunk.*        *(WARN Curtain.)*

RICHARD. *(Seriously)* Huh! You don't know her! *(Sinks back in chair)* Think I could fall in love with a girl that was afraid to say her soul's her own? I should say not! *(Then more gleefully still. Eagerly and dramatically leans to her)* And she's going to try and sneak out and meet me tonight. She says she thinks she can do it. *(Then suddenly, feeling this enthusiasm before* MILDRED *is entirely the wrong note for a cynical pessimist—with an affected bitter laugh, leans back in chair.* SID *half opens eyes—then goes back to sleep.)* Ha! I knew darned well she couldn't hold out—that she'd ask me again. *(He misquotes cynically)* "Women never know when the curtain has fallen. They always want another act."

MILDRED. *(Huffily)* Is that so, smarty?

RICHARD. *(Then as if he were weighing the matter. Overlap)* I don't know whether I'll consent to keep this date or not.

MILDRED. *(Lift)* Well, *I* know! You're not allowed out, you silly! So you can't!

RICHARD. *(Dropping all pretenses—defiantly)* Can't I, though! You wait and see if I can't! I'll see her tonight if it's the last thing I ever do! I don't care how I'm punished after!

MILDRED. *(Admiringly)* Goodness! I never thought you had such nerve!

RICHARD. You promise to keep your face shut, Mid—until after I've left tonight—then you can tell

Pa and Ma where I've gone—I mean, if they're worrying I'm off like last night.

MILDRED. All right. Only you've got to do something for me when I ask.

RICHARD. *(Overlap cue—Tempo)* Course I will. *(Excitedly)* And say, Mid, right now's the best chance for me to get away—while everyone's out. Ma'll be coming back soon and she'll keep watching me like a cat. *(Rises and starts for door* L.C.*)* I'm going now—I'll beat it upstairs and get dressed.

MILDRED. *(Rises and runs to* R. *of him)* But what will you do till night time—it's ages to wait?

RICHARD. What do I care how long I wait! *(With passionate intensity—away from* MILDRED*)* I'd wait a million years and never mind it—for her! *(To* MILDRED, *with superior scornful look)* The trouble with you is—you don't understand what love means. *(He exits* L.C.*)*

## FAST CURTAIN

## ACT THREE

### SCENE II

SCENE: *A strip of beach along the harbor. At Right, a bank of dark earth, running half-diagonally back along the beach, rises abruptly like a step a foot high marking the line where the sand of the beach ends and fertile land begins. The top of the bank is grassy and the trailing boughs of willow trees extend out over it and over a part of the beach. At Right Center is a path leading up the bank, between the willows. On the beach, at just Left of Center, a white, flat-bottomed rowboat is drawn up, its bow about touching the*

*bank, the painter trailing up the bank, evidently
made fast to the trunk of a willow. The new
moon casts a soft, mysterious, caressing light
over everything. The willows Right and the sand
Right are almost lost in shadows. And the willows fade into shadows off up Left. The last of
the path is in very pale moonlight which in-
creases as you walk downstage and toward the
Left to the boat, which is the high spot of the
moonlight. The boat is turned bottom up and is
directly across stage with the heavy rope attached
to the bow drawn tightly into the willows. The
sand of the beach shimmers palely. In the distance, the orchestra of a summer hotel can be
heard very faintly at intervals.*

DISCOVERED: *At rise,* RICHARD *is discovered sitting
sideways on the gunwale of the rowboat near the
stern. He is facing Right, watching the path. He
is in a great nervous state of anxious expectancy,
squirming about uncomfortably on the narrow
gunwale, kicking at the sand restlessly, twirling
his straw hat, with a bright-colored band in
stripes, around on his finger.*

RICHARD. *(Thinking)* Gosh, that music from the
hotel sounds wonderful. Must be nearly nine— I can
hear the Town Hall clock strike, it's so still tonight—
I'll catch hell when I get back, but it'll be worth it.
If only Muriel turns up— Am I sure she wrote
nine? *(He puts the straw hat on the sand* R. *of boat
and pulls the folded letter out of his pocket and peers
at it in the moonlight)* Yes, it's nine, all right. *(He
starts to put the note back in his pocket, then stops
and kisses it—then shoves it away hastily, sheepishly,
looking around him shamefacedly, as if afraid he
were being observed)* Aw, that's silly—no, it isn't
either—not when you're really in love— *(He jumps*

*to his feet restlessly)* Darn it, I wish she'd show up!
—think of something else—that'll make the time pass
quicker— *(Sits again on boat)* Last night?—the
Pleasant Beach House—Belle—ah, forget her!—
now, when Muriel's coming—that's a fine time to
think of—! But I didn't go upstairs with her—even
if she was pretty— Aw, she wasn't pretty— She
was just a whore— She was everything dirty—
Muriel's a million times prettier, anyway— Muriel
and I will go upstairs—when we're married—but that
will be *beautiful*— But I oughtn't even to think of
that yet—it's not right— I'd never—now—but after
we're married— *(He gives a little shiver of passionate longing—then resolutely turns his mind away
from these improper, almost desecrating thoughts)*
                                    *(WARN Clock.)*
That damned barkeep kicking me— I'll bet you if
I hadn't been drunk I'd have given him one good
punch in the nose— *(Then with a shiver of shamefaced revulsion and self-disgust)* Aw, you deserved
a kick in the pants—making such a darned slob of
yourself! You must have been a fine sight when you
got home!—having to be put to bed and getting sick!
Phaw! *(He squirms disgustedly)* Think of something else, can't you? Recite something— See if you
remember—
"Nay, let us walk from fire unto fire,
  From passionate pain to deadlier delight,
  I am too young to live without desire,
  Too young art thou to waste this summer night—"
*(Leans back on his arms)* Gee, that's a peach! I'll
have to memorize the rest and recite it to Muriel the
next time— I wish I could write poetry—about her
and me— *(He sighs and stares around him at the
night)* Gee, it's beautiful tonight—as if it was a
special night—for me and Muriel— Gee, I love tonight— I love the sand, and the trees, and the grass,
and the water, and the sky, and the moon— It's all

in me and I'm in it— God, it's so beautiful! *(He stares at the moon with a rapt face. From the distance the Town Hall CLOCK begins to strike. After the second gong strikes* RICHARD *hears it and it brings him back to earth with a start. CLOCK strikes nine.)* There's nine now— *(He rises and he peers at the path apprehensively)* I don't see her— She must have got caught. *(Almost tearfully)* Gee, I hate to go home and catch hell—without having seen her! *(Then calling a manly cynicism to his aid)* Aw, who ever heard of a woman being on time— *(Facing path)* I ought to know enough about life by this time not to expect— *(Then, with sudden excitement)* There she comes now— Gosh! *(He heaves a huge sigh of relief—then recites dramatically to himself, his eyes on the approaching figure)* "And lo, my love, mine own soul's heart—" *(Then hastily he crosses to down extreme* L.) Mustn't let her know I'm so tickled— If women are too sure of you, they treat you like slaves. Let her suffer for a change— *(He faces down* L. *with exaggerated carelessness, turning his back on the path, hands in pockets, whistling with insouciance "Waiting at the Church."* MURIEL MCCOMBER *enters from down the path up* R.C. *She is fifteen, going on sixteen. She is a pretty girl with a plump, graceful little figure, fluffy, light-brown hair, big naive wondering dark eyes, a round dimpled face, a soft melting drawly voice. Just now she is in a great thrilled state of timid adventurousness. She hesitates in the shadow at the foot of the path, waiting for* RICHARD *to see her, but he resolutely goes on whistling with back turned, and she has to call him.)*

MURIEL. Oh, Dick.

RICHARD. *(Turns around with an elaborate simulation of being disturbed in the midst of profound meditation. Assumed boredom)* Oh, hello. Is it nine already?

MURIEL. *(Coming toward him as far as the edge of the shadow—disappointedly)* I thought you'd be waiting right here at the end of the path. I'll bet you'd forgotten I was even coming.

RICHARD. *(Strolling a little toward her but not too far—carelessly)* No, I hadn't forgotten, honest. *(Seriously)* But I got to thinking about life. *(He is* **R.** *of bow of boat and below it.)*

MURIEL. *(Piqued)* You might think of me for a change. *(Hesitating timidly on the edge of the shadow, and then edges* R. *into deeper shadows)* Dick! You come here to me. I'm afraid to go out there where anyone might see me.

RICHARD. *(Coming toward her—scornfully)* Aw, there you go again—always scared of life!

MURIEL. *(Indignantly)* Dick Miller, I do think you've got an awful nerve to say that after all the risks I've run making this date and then sneaking out! You didn't take the trouble to sneak any letter to me, I notice!

RICHARD. *(Darkly)* No, because after your first letter, I thought everything was dead and past between us.

MURIEL. *(Woundedly)* And I'll bet you didn't care one little bit! *(On the verge of humiliated tears)* Oh, I was a fool ever to come here! I've got a good notion to go right home and never speak to you again! *(She half turns back toward the path.)*

RICHARD. *(Frightened—immediately becomes terribly sincere—grabbing her by the shoulders. They then cross to down* R.C.) Aw, don't go, Muriel! Please! I didn't mean anything like that, honest I didn't! Gee, if you knew how broken-hearted I was by that first letter, and how darned happy your second letter made me—!

MURIEL. *(Happily relieved—but appreciates she has the upper hand now and doesn't relent at once.*

*Faces him)* I don't believe you! You've got to swear to me.

RICHARD. I swear!

MURIEL. *(Demurely)* Well, then, all right, I'll believe you.

RICHARD. *(His eyes on her face lovingly—genuine adoration in his voice)* Gosh, you're pretty tonight, Muriel! It seems ages since we've been together. Gosh, Muriel, it sure is wonderful to be with you again! *(He puts a timid hand on her shoulder, awkwardly.)*

MURIEL. *(Shyly)* I'm glad—it makes you happy. I'm happy, too.

RICHARD. *(Stammering timidly)* Can't I—won't you let me kiss you—now? Please! *(He bends his face toward hers.)*

MURIEL. *(Ducking her head away—timidly)* No! You mustn't. Don't—

RICHARD. Aw, why can't I? Aren't you ever going to let me?

MURIEL. I will—sometime.

RICHARD. When?

MURIEL. Soon, maybe.

RICHARD. Tonight, will you?

MURIEL. *(Coyly)* I'll see.

RICHARD. Promise?

MURIEL. I promise—maybe.

RICHARD. All right. You remember you've promised. *(Then coaxingly)* Aw, don't let's stand here. Come on out and we can sit down in the boat.

MURIEL. *(Can't resist this)* Well, all right— *(She lets him lead her toward the boat. They sit on the left end of the boat. RICHARD L. of MURIEL.)* Only I can't stay only a few minutes.

RICHARD. *(Frightened at the idea of losing her—pleadingly)* Aw, you can stay a little while, can't you? **Please!**

MURIEL. A little while. But I've got to be home in bed again pretending to be asleep by ten o'clock.

RICHARD. But you'll have lots of time to do that.

MURIEL. *(Excitedly)* Dick, you have no idea what I went through to get here tonight! My, but it was exciting! I had to get all undressed and into bed and Ma came up, and I pretended to be asleep, and she went down again, and I got up and dressed in such a hurry— I must look a sight, don't I?

RICHARD. You do not. You look wonderful.

MURIEL. *(She likes this. But then dramatizes her experiences)* And then I sneaked down the back stairs. *(Then reproachfully)* Dick, you don't realize how I've been punished for your sake.

RICHARD. *(Importantly)* And *you* don't realize what I've been through for you—and what I'm in for —for sneaking out tonight—and staying away all day— *(Then darkly)* And for what I did last night —what your letter made me do!

MURIEL. *(Made terribly curious by his ominous tone)* What did my letter make you do?

RICHARD. *(Beginning to glory in this—darkly)* It's too long a story—"and let the dead past bury its dead." *(Then with real feeling)* Only it isn't past, I can *tell you!* What I'll catch when Pa gets hold of me!

MURIEL. Tell me, Dick! Begin at the beginning and tell me!

RICHARD. *(Tragically)* Well, after your old—your father left our place I caught holy hell from Pa.

MURIEL. *(Shocked)* Dick! You mustn't swear!

RICHARD. *(Darkly)* Hell is the only word that can describe it. And on top of that, to torture me more, he gave me your letter.

MURIEL. *(Touched)* I'm so awful sorry, Dick— honest I am!

RICHARD. I thought your love for me was dead.

I wanted to die. I sat and brooded about death.
Finally I made up my mind I'd kill myself.

MURIEL. *(Excitedly)* Dick! You didn't!

RICHARD. I did, too! If there'd been one of Hedda
Gabler's pistols around, you'd have seen if I wouldn't
have done it beautifully. I thought, "When I'm
dead, she'll be sorry she ruined my life!"

MURIEL. *(Cuddling up a little to him)* If you ever
had! I'd have died, too! Honest, I would!

RICHARD. But suicide is the act of a coward. *(Then
with a bitter change of tone)* And anyway, I thought
to myself, she isn't worth it!

MURIEL. *(Huffily)* That's a nice thing to say!

RICHARD. Well, if you meant what was in that
letter you wouldn't have been worth it, would you?

MURIEL. But I've told you, Pa—

RICHARD. *(Overlap cue)* So I said to myself, "I'm
through with women; they're all alike—"

MURIEL. I'm not.

RICHARD. *(Dramatic)* And I thought, "What
difference does it make what I do now; I might as
well forget her and lead the pace that kills, and drown
my sorrows!" *(Sincerely)* You know, I had eleven
dollars saved up to buy you something for your birth-
day, but I thought: *(Dramatic)* "She's dead to me
now and why shouldn't I throw it away?" *(Then
hastily and sincerely)* I've still got almost five left,
Muriel, and I can get you something nice with that.

MURIEL. *(Excitedly)* What do I care about your
old presents? You tell me what you did!

RICHARD. *(Darkly again)* After it was dark, I
sneaked out and went to a *low dive* I know about.

MURIEL. Dick Miller, I don't believe you ever!

RICHARD. You ask them at the Pleasant Beach
House if I didn't! They won't forget me in a hurry!

MURIEL. *(Impressed and horrified)* Why, that's
a terrible place! Pa says it ought to be closed by the
police!

RICHARD. *(Darkly)* I said it was a dive, didn't I? It's a "secret house of shame." And they let me into a *secret* room behind the barroom. There wasn't anyone there but a Princeton Senior I know—he belongs *to Tiger Inn* and he's *fullback* on the *football team*—and he had two chorus girls from New York with him, and they were all drinking *champagne.*

MURIEL. *(Disturbed by the entrance of the chorus girls)* Dick Miller! I hope you didn't notice—

RICHARD. *(Carelessly. Elaborate a bit—glances at* MURIEL *to see how she takes it)* I noticed one of the girls—the one that wasn't with him—looking at me. She had strange-looking eyes. *(Lift)* And then she asked me if I wouldn't drink champagne with them and come and *sit* with her.

MURIEL. She must have been a nice thing!

RICHARD. *(Then rubbing it in)* Her name was Belle. She had golden hair—the kind that burns and stings you.

MURIEL. I'll bet it was dyed!

RICHARD. She kept smoking one cigarette after another—but that's nothing for a chorus girl.

MURIEL. *(Indignantly. Away from him)* She was low and bad; that's what she was or she couldn't be a chorus girl, and her smoking cigarettes proves it! *(Then falteringly again to him)* And then what happened?

RICHARD. *(Carelessly)* Oh, we just kept drinking champagne—*(Point this a bit.)*—and then I had a fight with the barkeep and knocked him down because he'd insulted her.

MURIEL. *(Huffily. Away from him)* I don't see how he could insult that kind! *(To him)* And why did you fight for her? Why didn't the Princeton fullback—

RICHARD. *(Slightly hesitant)* He was too drunk by that time.

MURIEL. And were you drunk?

RICHARD. Only a *little* then. I was worse later. You ought to have seen me when I got home! *(With great pria?)* I was on the verge of delirium tremens!

MURIEL. I'm glad I didn't see you. I hate people who get drunk! I'd have hated you! *(Then faltering but fascinated)* But what happened with that Belle—after—before you went home?

RICHARD. Oh, we kept drinking champagne and she came and sat on my lap and kissed me.

MURIEL. *(Stiffening with almost a sob)* Oh!

RICHARD. *(Quickly, afraid he has gone too far)* But it was only all in fun.

MURIEL. And did you kiss her?

RICHARD. No, I didn't.

MURIEL. *(Distractedly. To him)* You did, too! You're lying and you know it. *(Then tearfully. Dramatize three-fourths front)* And here *I* was, right at that time, lying in bed not able to sleep, wondering how I was ever going to see you again and crying my eyes out, while you—! *(She suddenly jumps to her feet in a tearful fury—faces him)* I hate you! I wish you were dead! I never want to lay eyes on you again! And this time I mean it! *(She turns to leave. He grabs her left hand in both of his and holds her back. All the pose has dropped from him now and he is in a terrible state of contrition and fear of losing her—remains seated on boat.)*

RICHARD. *(Imploringly)* Muriel! Wait! Listen!

MURIEL. *(Facing front)* I don't want to listen! Let me go! If you don't I'll bite your hand!

RICHARD. I won't let you go! You've got to let me explain! I never—! *(For MURIEL has bitten his hand and it hurts, and, stung by the pain, he lets go instinctively and jumps to his feet. She immediately starts running toward the path. RICHARD calls after her with bitter despair and hurt)* All right: Go if you want to—if you haven't the decency to let me explain. I hate you, too! I'll go and see Belle!

MURIEL. *(Stops at foot of the path as soon as* RICHARD *speaks. Remains facing upstage until she speaks, then turns on him)* Well, go and see her—if that's the kind of girl you like! What do I care? (RICHARD *sits* L. *end of boat. Then as he only stares before him broodingly, sitting dejectedly in the stern of the boat, a pathetic figure of injured grief—she drifts a step toward him and then speaks)* You can't explain! What can you explain! You owned up you kissed her!

RICHARD. I did not. I said she kissed me.

MURIEL. *(Scornfully, but drifting back a step in his direction)* And I suppose you just sat and let yourself be kissed! Tell that to the Marines!

RICHARD. *(Injuredly)* All right! If you're going to call me a liar every word I say— (MURIEL *drifts back another step. Then suddenly defiant)* And what if I did kiss her once or twice? I only did it to get back at you!

MURIEL. Dick!

RICHARD. You're a fine one to blame me—when it was all your fault! Didn't I think you were out of my life forever? Hadn't you written me you were? Answer me that!

MURIEL. But I've told you a million times that Pa stood right over me and told me each word to write. I had to pretend, so I'd get a chance to see you. Don't you see, silly? *(He doesn't answer. She moves nearer down* R.C.) Still, I can see how you felt the way you did—and maybe I *am* to blame for that. So I'll forgive and forget, Dick—if you'll swear to me you didn't even think of loving that—

RICHARD. *(Eagerly)* I didn't! I swear, Muriel. I couldn't. I love you!

MURIEL. Well, then—I still love you.

RICHARD. Then come back *here*, why don't you?

MURIEL. *(Comes back and sits down by him shyly)* All right—only I'll have to go soon, Dick. *(He*

*puts his arm around her waist. She cuddles up close
to him—taking his right hand which is about her
waist)* I'm sorry—I hurt your hand.

RICHARD. That was nothing. It felt wonderful even
to have you bite.

MURIEL. *(Impulsively she kisses his hand)* There!
That'll cure it. *(She is overcome by confusion at her
boldness.)*

RICHARD. You shouldn't—waste that—on my hand.
*(Then tremblingly)* You said—you'd let me—

MURIEL. Will it wash off—her kisses—make you
forget you ever—for always?

RICHARD. I should say so! I'd never remember
anything about it—ever again.

MURIEL. *(Shyly lifting her lips)* Then—all right—
Dick. *(He kisses her tremblingly and for a moment
their lips remain together. Then she lets her head
sink on his shoulder and sighs softly)* The moon is
beautiful, isn't it?

RICHARD. *(Kissing her hair)* Not as beautiful as
you. Nothing is! *(Then after a pause)* Won't it be
wonderful when we're married?

MURIEL. Yes—but it's so long to wait.

RICHARD. Perhaps I needn't go to Yale. Perhaps
Pa will give me a job. Then I'd soon be making
enough to—

MURIEL. You better do what your Pa thinks best
—and I'd like you to be at Yale. *(Then taking his
hand)* Poor you! Do you think he'll punish you
awful? *(WARN Curtain.)*

RICHARD. *(With intense sincerity)* I don't know
and I don't care! Nothing would have kept me from
seeing you tonight—not if I'd have to crawl over
red-hot coals! *(Then lapsing into literary Swinburn-
ian passion)* You are my love, mine own soul's heart,
more dear than mine own soul, more beautiful than
God!

MURIEL. *(Shocked and delighted)* Ssshh! It's wrong to say that!

RICHARD. *(His passionate devotion crying out in the commonplace—intensely and adoringly)* Gosh, but I love you! *(She sinks into his arms again)* Gosh, I love you—Darling!

MURIEL. *(Lifting her lips to his)* I love you, too —Sweetheart! *(They kiss. Then she lets her head sink on his shoulder again and they both sit in rapt trance, staring at the moon. After a pause—dreamily)* Where'll we go on our honeymoon, Dick? To Niagara Falls?

RICHARD. *(Scornfully and abruptly)* That dump where all the silly fools go? I should say not! *(With a passionately earnest romanticism)* No, we'll go to some far-off wonderful place! *(He calls on Kipling to help him)* Somewhere out on the Long Trail— the trail that is always new— On the road to Mandalay! We'll watch the dawn come up like thunder out of China!

MURIEL. *(Hastily but happily)* That'll be wonderful, won't it?

## FAST CURTAIN

## ACT THREE

### SCENE III

SCENE: *The sitting-room of the Miller house again —around ten o'clock the same night.* MILLER *is sitting in chair #3, his wife in chair #1. Moonlight shines faintly through the screen door up* L. *Only the green-shaded reading lamp is lit and by its light,* MILLER, *his specs on, is reading a book while his wife, sewing basket*

*in lap, is working industriously on a doily.* MRS.
MILLER'S *face wears an expression of unworried
content.* MILLER'S *face has also lost its look of
harassed preoccupation, although he still is a
prey to certain misgivings, when he allows himself to think of them. Several books are piled
on the table by his elbow, the books that have
been confiscated from* RICHARD.

MILLER. *(Chuckles at something he reads—then
closes the book and puts it on the table.* MRS. MILLER
*looks up from her sewing.)* This Shaw's a comical
cuss—even if his ideas are so crazy they oughtn't
to allow them to be printed.

MRS. MILLER. *(Smiling teasingly)* I can see where
you're becoming corrupted by those books, too—pretending to read them out of duty to Richard, when
your nose has been glued to the page!

MILLER. No, no—but I've got to be honest. There's
something to them. That "Rubaiyat of Omar Khay-
yam," now. I read that over again and liked it even
better than I had before—

MRS. MILLER. *(Has been busy with her own
thoughts during this last—with a deep sigh of relief)*
My, but I'm glad Mildred told me where Richard's
gone. I'd have worried my heart out if she hadn't.
But now it's all right.

MILLER. *(Frowning a little)* I'd hardly go so far
as to say that. Just because we know he's all right
tonight doesn't mean last night is wiped out. He's
still got to be punished for that.

MRS. MILLER. *(Defensively)* Well, if you ask me,
I think after the way I punished him all day, and the
way I know he's punished himself, he's had about
all he deserves. I've told you how sorry he was, and
how he said he'd never touch liquor again. He hated
the taste of it, and it didn't make him feel happy like

Sid, but only sad and sick, so he didn't see anything in it for him.

MILLER. *(With satisfaction)* Well, if he's really got that view of it driven into his skull, I don't know but I'm glad it all happened. That'll protect him more than a *thousand* lectures—just horse sense about himself. *(Then frowning again)* Still, I can't let him do such things and go scot-free. No, he's got to be punished, if only to make the lesson stick in his mind, and I'm going to tell him he can't go to Yale, seeing he's so undependable.

MRS. MILLER. *(Up in arms at once. Scold angrily —build)* Not go to Yale! I guess he can go to Yale! If our other children can get the benefit of a college education, you're not going to pick on Richard—

MILLER. *(Irritably, at last breaking through her eloquence)* Hush up, for God's sake! If you'd let me finish, I said I'd *tell* him that now—bluff—then later on I'll change my mind, if he behaves himself.

MRS. MILLER. *(Relieved)* Oh, well, if that's all— *(Then defensively again)* But it's your duty to give him every benefit. He's got an exceptional brain, that boy has! He's proved it by the way he likes to read all those deep plays and poetry.

MILLER. But I thought you— *(He stops abruptly, grinning helplessly.)*

MRS. MILLER. *(Challengingly)* You thought I what?

MILLER. Never mind.

MRS. MILLER. *(Sniffs, but thinks it better to let this pass)* You mark my words, that boy's going to turn out to be a great lawyer, or a great doctor, or a great writer, or—

MILLER. *(Grinning)* You agree he's going to be great, anyway.

MRS. MILLER. Yes, I most certainly have a lot of faith in Richard.

MILLER. *(Picks up book and opens it)* Well, so
have I, as far as that goes.

MRS. MILLER. And as for his being in love with
Muriel! I don't see but what it might work out real
well. *(Lift lightly)* Richard could do worse.

MILLER. *(Kids her a little)* But I thought you had
no use for Muriel, thought she was stupid—

MRS. MILLER. Well, so I did, but if she's good for
Richard and he wants her— *(Then inconsequentially)*
Ma used to say you weren't over bright—(MILLER
*grins "Oh.")*—but she changed her mind when she
saw I didn't care if you were or not.

MILLER. *(Not exactly pleased by this—huffily)*
Well, I've been bright enough to—

MRS. MILLER. *(Going on as if he had not spoken.
Brightly and quickly)* And Muriel's real cute-looking,
I have to admit that. Takes after her mother. Alice
Briggs was the the prettiest girl before she married!

MILLER. Yes, and Muriel will get big as a house
after *she's* married, the same as her mother did.
That's the trouble. A man never can tell what he's
letting himself in— *(He stops, feeling his wife's
eyes fixed on him with indignant suspicion.)*

MRS. MILLER. *(Sharply. Faces* MILLER*)* I'm not
too fat and don't you say it!

MILLER. *(Chuckles)* Who was talking about you?
*(Flatteringly)* Why, no one'd ever call you fat,
Esssie. You're only plump, like a good figure ought
to be.

MRS. MILLER. *(Pleased but embarrassed)* Crazy.
*(She then laughs—quite pleased.)*

MILLER. *(After a moment he turns to* MRS. MILLER
*seriously)* You don't mean to tell me you're actually
taking this Muriel crush of Richard's seriously, do
you? I know it's a good thing to encourage right
now but—pshaw, why, Richard'll probably forget all
about her before he's away six months and she'll have
forgotten him.

MRS. MILLER. *(Rebukingly. Sharply)* Don't be so cynical. *(Then, after a pause, thoughtfully)* Well, anyway, he'll always have it to remember—no matter what happens after—and that's something.

MILLER. You *bet* that's something. *(Then with a grin)* You surprise me at times with your deep wisdom!

MRS. MILLER. *(Quickly)* You don't give me credit for ever having common sense, that's why. *(She goes back to her sewing.)*

MILLER. *(After a pause)* Where'd you say Sid and Lily had gone off to?

MRS. MILLER. To the beach to listen to the band. *(She sighs sympathetically)* Poor Lily! Sid'll never change, and she'll never marry him. But she seems to get some queer satisfaction out of fussing over him.

MILLER. Arthur's up with Elsie Rand, I suppose?

MRS. MILLER. Of course.

MILLER. Where's Mildred?

MRS. MILLER. Out walking with her latest. I've forgot who it is. I can't keep track of them. *(She smiles.)*

MILLER. *(Smiling)* Then, from all reports, we seem to be completely surrounded by love!

MRS. MILLER. Well, we've had our share, haven't we? We don't have to begrudge it to our children. *(Then has a sudden thought)* But I've done all this talking about Muriel and Richard and clean forgot how wild old McComber was against it. But he'll get over that, I suppose.

MILLER. *(With satisfaction)* He has already. I ran into him upstreet this afternoon and he was meek as pie. He backed water and said he guessed I was right. Richard had just copied stuff out of books, and kids would be kids, and so on. So I came off my high horse a bit—but not too far—and I guess all that won't bother anyone any more. *(Chuckles. Then rubbing his hands together—with a boyish grin of pleasure)* And I told you about getting that business from Lawson, didn't I? It's been a good day, Essie —a darned good day! *(From off up L. is heard the FOOTSTEPS of someone coming around the piazza to the side door. MRS. MILLER looks up from her sewing, listening a moment.)*

MRS. MILLER. *(In a whisper)* It's Richard.

MILLER. *(Immediately assuming an expression of becoming gravity)* Hmm. *(He takes off his spectacles and puts them back in their case and straightens himself in his chair. RICHARD comes slowly in through the up L. door, which is open. He walks like one in a trance, his eyes shining with a dreamy happiness, his spirit still too exalted to be conscious of his surroundings, or to remember the threatened punishment. He carries his straw hat dangling in his hand, quite unaware of its existence. Crosses slowly to sofa down R. via below table R.)*

RICHARD. *(Dreamily, like a ghost addressing fellow shades. After he has crossed to sofa and is seated he leans forward on his elbows as he says in a breathy voice)* Hello.

MRS. MILLER. *(Staring at him worriedly)* Hello, Richard.

MILLER. *(Sizing him up shrewdly)* Hello, Son.

MRS. MILLER. *(With frightened suspicion now)* Goodness, he acts queer! Nat you don't suppose he's been—? *(She looks.)*

MILLER. *(With a reassuring smile)* No. It's love, not liquor, this time.

MRS. MILLER. *(Only partly reassured—rises; crosses to L. of RICHARD—then speaks sharply)* Richard! What's the matter with you? *(He comes to himself with a start. She goes on scoldingly)* How many times have I told you to hang up your hat in the hall when you come in! *(He looks at his hat as if he were surprised at its existence.)* Here. Give it to me. *(She snatches it out of his hand and starts to put it away in hall off* L.C., *crossing via above table* R. MILLER *speaks to her as she starts to move away from* RICHARD.)

MILLER. *(Quietly but firmly now)* Essie! You better leave Richard and me alone for a while, Essie. (RICHARD *rises; stands down extreme* R., *facing his father.)*

MRS. MILLER. *(Turns to stare at him apprehensively)* Well—all right—I'll go sit on the piazza. Call me if you want me. *(Then. a bit pleadingly)* But you'll remember all I've said, Nat, won't you? (MILLER *nods reassuringly. She disappears off* L.C. RICHARD, *keenly conscious of himself as the about-to-be-sentenced criminal by this time, looks guilty and a bit defiant, searches his father's expressionless face with uneasy side glances, and steels himself for what is coming.)*

MILLER. *(Casually, indicating chair* #1) Sit down, Richard. (RICHARD *slumps awkwardly into the chair* #1 *and sits in a self-conscious, unnatural position.* MILLER *sizes him up keenly—then suddenly smiles and asks with quiet mockery)* Well, how are the vine leaves in your hair this evening?

RICHARD. *(Totally unprepared for this approach, shamefacedly mutters)* I don't know, Pa.

MILLER. Turned out to be poison ivy, didn't they? *(Then kindly)* But you needn't look so alarmed. I'm not going to read you any temperance lecture. That'd bore me more than it would you. And, in spite of your damn foolishness last night, I'm still giving you credit for having brains. So I'm pretty sure anything I could say to you you've already said to yourself.

RICHARD. *(His head down—humbly)* I know I was a darned fool.

MILLER. *(Thinking it well to rub in this aspect—disgustedly)* You sure were—not only a fool but a downright, stupid, disgusting fool! (RICHARD

*squirms, his head still lower.)* It was bad enough for
you to let me and Arthur see you, but to appear like
that before your mother and Mildred—! And I wonder if Muriel would think you were so fine if she ever
saw you as you looked and acted then. I think she'd
give you your walking papers for keeps. And you
couldn't blame her. No nice girl wants to give her
love to a stupid drunk!

RICHARD. *(Crimson and writhing)* I know, Pa.

MILLER. *(After a pause—quietly but definitely)*
All right. Then that settles the booze end of it. *(He
sizes RICHARD up searchingly—then suddenly speaks
sharply)* But there is another thing that's more
serious. *(Rises; comes down to chair #4; sits; leans
over table)* How about that tart you went to bed with
at the Pleasant Beach House?

RICHARD. *(Flabbergasted—stammers)* You know?
*(A moment before RICHARD continues. MILLER re-
acts—thinks the boy has admitted guilt; looks away
from him, hurt.)* But I didn't! (MILLER *reacts; looks
quickly and searchingly at* RICHARD.) If they've told
you about her down there, they must have told you I
didn't! I gave her the five dollars just so she'd let
me out of it. She made everything seem rotten and
dirty—and—I didn't want to do a thing like that to
Muriel—no matter how bad I thought she'd treated
me—even after I felt drunk, I didn't. Honest!

MILLER. How'd you happen to meet this lady, anyway?

RICHARD. I can't tell that, Pa. I'd have to snitch
on someone—and you wouldn't want me to do that.

MILLER. *(A bit taken back)* No, I suppose I
wouldn't. Hmm. Well, I believe you—and I guess
that settles that. *(Then, after a quick, furtive glance
at RICHARD, he nerves himself for the ordeal and begins with a shamefaced, self-conscious solemnity.
Rises and crosses R.; looks about room)* But listen
here, Richard—hmm—it's about time you and I had

a serious talk about—hmm—certain matters pertain-
ing to—and now that the subject's come up of its
own accord, it's a good time—I mean, there's no use
in procrastinating further—so, here goes. *(But it
doesn't go smoothly, and as he goes on he becomes
more and more guiltily embarrassed and self-conscious and his expression more stilted.* RICHARD
*sedulously avoids even glancing at him, his own em-
barrassment made tenfold more painful by his father's. Slaps* RICHARD *on the back affectionately—then
says with gusto)* Richard— *(Crosses to chair #4
and sits)* —you have now come to the age when—
well, you're a fully developed man, in a way—and
it's only natural for you to have certain—hmm—
desires of the flesh, to put it that way—I mean, per-
taining to the opposite sex—hmm—certain natural
feelings and temptations—that'll wan. to be gratified
—and you'll want to gratify them. *(New attack)*
Well, there are a certain class of women—always
have been and always will be as long as human nature
is what it is— *(Excuses)* It's wrong, maybe, but
what can you do about it? I mean, girls like that one
you— *(Looks about room quickly to be sure no one
will hear this)* —girls there's something doing with
—and lots of 'em are pretty, and it's human nature if
you— But that doesn't mean to ever get mixed up
with them seriously! Don't think I'm encouraging
you to— If you can stay away from 'em, all the
better—but if—why—hmm— Here's what I'm driving at, Richard. They're apt to be whited sepulchres.
I mean, your whole life might be ruined if—so, darn
it, you've got to know how to—I mean, there are
ways and means— *(Suddenly he can go no farther
and explodes helplessly)* But, hell, I suppose you boys
talk this over among yourselves and you know more
about it than I do. I'll admit I'm no authority.
*(Speaks now with serious strength and force—driv-
ing home his advice)* I never had anything to do with

such women, and it'll be a hell of a lot better for you if you never do!

RICHARD. *(Without looking at him. Quietly)* I'm never going to, Pa. *(Then shocked indignation coming into his voice—looks at* MILLER) I don't see how you could think I could—now—when you know I love Muriel and am going to marry her. I'd die before I'd—!

MILLER. *(Immensely relieved—enthusiastically rises)* That's the talk! By God, I'm proud of you when you talk like that! *(Then hastily)* And now that's all of that. *(Crosses to* RICHARD) There's nothing more to say and we'll forget it, eh? *(Slaps him on neck affectionately. Crosses down* L.C. *to up* L. *and then down* L. *After a pause.)*

RICHARD. Oh, Pa.

MILLER. *(Blowing his nose as he crosses to down* L.) Huh?

RICHARD. How are you going to punish me, Pa?

MILLER. *(Smiling—crosses to* L. *of him)* I *was* sort of forgetting that, wasn't I? Well, I'd thought of telling you you couldn't go to Yale—

RICHARD. *(Eagerly—jumps to his feet)* Don't I have to go? Gee, that's great! Muriel thought you'd want me to. I was telling her I'd rather you gave me a job on the paper because then she and I could get married sooner. *(Then with a boyish grin—sits on the* R. *arm of chair* #1) Gee, Pa, you picked a lemon. *(Laughs)* That isn't any punishment. You'll have to do something besides that.

MILLER. *(Grimly—but only half concealing an answering grin. Crosses to* RICHARD—*angrily)* Then you'll go to Yale and you'll stay there till you graduate, that's that answer to that! Muriel's got good sense and you haven't! (RICHARD *accepts this philosophically.)* And now we're finished. You better call your mother. *(Crosses to up* C. RICHARD *crosses to up* L *and calls "Ma," toward screen door, and a moment later she comes in through screen door, leaving it open behind her. She glances quickly from son to husband and immediately knows that all is well, and tactfully refrains from all questions.)*

MRS. MILLER. *(Crosses to desk chair. Relieved and speaks lightly)* My, it's a beautiful night. The moon's way down low—almost setting. *(She sits in her chair and sighs contentedly.* RICHARD *remains standing by the door, staring out at the moon, his face pale in the moonlight.)*

MILLER. *(Standing below table* R. *With a nod at* RICHARD, *winking at his wife)* Yes, I don't believe I've hardly ever seen such a beautiful night—with such a wonderful moon. Have you, Richard?

RICHARD. *(Turning to them—enthusiastically. Crosses down* C. *a step)* No! It was wonderful—down at the beach— *(He stops abruptly, smiling shyly.)*

MILLER. *(Watching his son strangely—quietly)* No, I can only remember a few nights that were as beautiful as this—and they were long ago when your mother and I were young and planning to get married.

RICHARD. *(Stares at them wonderingly for a moment, then quickly from his father to his mother and back again, strangely as if he'd never seen them before—but then suddenly his face is transfigured by a smile of understanding and sympathy. He speaks shyly, crossing down a step)* Yes, I'll bet those must have been wonderful nights, too. You sort of forget the moon was the same way back then—and everything.

MILLER. *(A trifle huskily. Crosses to him, pats him on the back, then speaks)* You're all right, Richard!

MRS. MILLER. *(Fondly)* You're a good boy, Richard. *(*RICHARD *looks dreadfully shy and embarrassed at this. His father comes to his rescue.)*

MILLER. Better get to bed early tonight, Son, hadn't you?

RICHARD. I couldn't sleep. Can't I go out on the piazza and sit for a while—until the moon sets?

MILLER. All right. Then you better say good night now. I don't know about your mother, but I'm going to bed right away. I'm dead tired. *(WARN lights.)*

MRS. MILLER. So am I.

RICHARD. *(Goes to her and kisses her)* Good night, Ma.

MRS. MILLER. Good night. Don't you stay up till all hours now.                                    *(WARN Curtain.)*

RICHARD. *(Comes to his father and stands awkwardly before him)* Good night, Pa.

MILLER. *(Puts him arms around him and gives him a hug)* Good night, Son. (Crosses a step down; faces front. RICHARD turns impulsively and kisses him—then hurries out up L. MILLER stares after him, then says huskily)* First time he's done that in years. I don't believe in kissing between fathers and sons after a certain age—seems mushy and silly—but that meant something! (Crosses to rear of the chair L.C. and faces MRS. MILLER, who is still seated on desk chair)* And I don't think we'll ever have to worry about his being safe!—from himself—again. And I guess no matter what life will do to him, he can take care of it now.

MRS. MILLER. *(Rises and crosses to lamp, which is above table R.)* Yes, Nat. I'm going to turn out the light. All ready?                                    *(LIGHTS.)*

MILLER. Yep. Let her go, Gallagher. *(She turns out the lamp. MILLER crosses to up L.C. and stands looking out of screen door. MRS. MILLER joins him and stands just below and right of him. In the ensuing darkness the faint MOONLIGHT shines full in through the screen door. Walking back together toward the front parlor they stand full in it for a moment, staring out.* MILLER *reaches out and puts his right arm around her and she puts her left arm around him. He says in a low voice, smilingly)* There he is—like a statue of Love's Young Dream. *(Then he sighs and she sighs. Then he speaks with a gentle nostalgic melancholy)* What's it that Rubaiyat says:

"Yet Ah, that Spring should vanish with the
     Rose!
 That Youth's sweet-scented manuscript should
     close!"

*(Then throwing off his melancholy with a loving smile at ner)* Well, Spring isn't everything, is it, Essie? There's a lot to be said for Autumn. Autumn's got beauty, too. And Winter—if you're together!

MRS. MILLER. *(Sirnly)* Yes, Nat. *(She kisses him and then they move quietly out of the moonlight into the darkness of the front parlor* L.C.*)*

## CURTAIN

# AH, WILDERNESS!

## PROPERTY PLOT

### ACT ONE

#### Scene I

Large sofa down extreme Right.

3 sofa cushions on sofa.

Large bookcase with glass doors against Right wall
    above sofa.

Books, various sets in large bookcase.

Square table in corner up Right.

Brass jardinier and Boston fern on square table.

Portieres for sliding doors in rear wall Right. Val-
    ance.

Bookcase without doors with practical books up Cen-
    ter.

Portieres for sliding doors in rear wall Left. Valance.

Side chair against rear wall, Left of double doors up
    Left.

Writing desk and desk chair against Left wall below
    screen door and above window in Left wall.

On desk:

    Writing pads of various sizes.

    Writing paper.

    Several pencils.

    Small whiskey glass filled with parlor matches.

    Ash tray on down stage end of desk.

    Sewing basket on top part of desk.

In sewing basket:
> Needles (one threaded).
> Several spools of white thread.
> A number of dish towels that need to be hemmed.

Large oval table, down stage below double doors R.
On oval table:
> Newspaper *(Nantucket Courier* is best for this).
> 5 magazines (1906).
> 1 1906 magazine light enough to be used as a fan.
> A small glass filled with parlor matches.
> Ashtray—a medium colored table throw.

Side chair down Left Center, on same level as desk
> chair.

Rocking chair down extreme Left, below desk, fac-
> ing upstage.

Armchair (chair #1) down Right of oval table.

Armchair (chair #2) up Right of oval table.

Rocking chair (chair #3) up Left of oval table.

Armchair (chair #4) down Left of oval table.

Rug covering most of floor.

Folding screen in backing up R.

Small square table (dressing piece) in backing up L.
On small square table:
> A sea shell (wired to table).
> A small vase (wired to table).
> A white linen cover.

On window down Right:
> 1 set of straight hanging, lace-net, sill length
> > curtains.
> 1 set of tie-back lace-net curtains, floor length.
> 1 set of brocade tie-back, floor length curtains
> > with valance (brown with gold braid (over)
> > and tassles).

On window down Left the same as window down
> Right.

One oval framed picture of flowers on a black back-
> ground over desk Left.

ARTHUR hand props:
> Tobacco pouch—watch and chain.
> Blue Boar Tobacco.
> Pipe with initials Y'o8 on it (large pipe).

MILLER hand props:
> Watch and chain.
> Cigar case.
> Five cigars.
> Spectacles with the "half-moon" lense.

DAVE McCOMBER hand props:
> Breast pocket wallet.
> 5 slips of paper with two verses written on them.
> > These are off up Left. Slips of paper must be small enough to fit into wallet.
> One sealed envelope containing a letter, off up Left.

SID hand props:
> Cigar off up Right.

LILY MILLER hand props:
> Pince nez (in sewing basket on desk).
> Small gold breast watch attached to the upper Left breast of her dress with a gold Fleur-de-lis pin or chatelaine.

RICHARD hand props:
> Book of Carlyle's French Revolution off up Right.

Noise effects:
> 3 twenty-two calibre blank pistols.
> 1 45 calibre pistol for the torpedo effect.
> (Noise to be off up Left).

## ACT ONE

### SCENE II

Small table above screen door down Right.
A potted "Rubber-plant."

Portieres for sliding doors in Right wall above small
table. Valance.

Narrow serving table against rear wall, Right of
pantry door. Seven dinner plates (lobster plates).
Lace runner.

Large heavy china-cabinet against rear wall, Center
of Left space between Left wall and the swinging door up c. On the shelves are the "fancy"
china of the family.

Large painting on wall over service table of a meadow
and a stream—the picture is in a gold frame.

Large painting on rear wall, Left of china cabinet, of
a meadow.

Sideboard against Left wall between windows.

Fancy linen runner.

Several silver pieces decorate the top of the sideboard.

One side chair down Left, facing front.

Dining-room table (4'6" x 6') below china cabinet.

7 napkins.

7 napkin rings.

7 water glasses.

1 table cloth.

1 silencer cloth.

Large cutglass water pitcher half filled with
water.

Cutglass olive dish with olives.

7 knives and forks.

7 tea spoons.

7 soup spoons.

7 lobster forks.

7 butter knives.

Large soup ladle—at Left end of table.

Serving silver for lobster, fish, vegetables.

2 sets of salt and peppers.

7 bread plates.

12 Parkerhouse rolls on large bread plate.

1 butter plate with ¼ pound of butter.

1 butter knife.
1 dish towel on R. end of table for MRS. MILLER.
7 soup plates on Left end of table.
7 fish plates on Right end of table.
Bowl of daisies off up R. for MRS. MILLER.
Large china soup tureen with cover—off up Center
    for NORA.
Dish of saltines off up Center for NORA.
1 vegetable dish with mashed potatoes.
1 vegetable dish of either peas, beans, carrots, etc.
1 platter of broiled bluefish off up Center for NORA.
1 platter of cold boiled lobster off up Center for
    NORA.
1 large red and gray rug covering most of the floor.

For windows in Left wall:
    1 set of brocade tie-back floor length curtains
        with red braid and tassels.
    1 set of reddish brown brocade tie-back curtains
        with red braid and tassels. Valance.
    1 set of lace-net tie-back curtains floor length.
    1 set of straight hanging lace-net sill-length cur-
        tains.
Armchair at Right end of table.
Armchair at Left end of table.
3 sidechairs upstage side of table.
2 sidechairs downstage side of table.


ACT TWO

SCENE I

Picture on upstage wall above player piano—hung at
    an angle. Picture is of ' Temptations."
3 round tables.
    One up Left.

One up Center, Right of door in rear wall.
One down Right Center.
9 wicker-seated chairs.
    One Left of each table.
    One Right of each table.
    One below table up Center.
    One above the other two tables.
3 brass cuspidors.
    One against Left wall in line with table up Left.
    One below the other two tables.
Gin-rickey glass (empty except for ice and a slice of
    lime on table up Left).
Half empty glass of beer on table up Left.
3 ash trays and match holders (parlor matches).
    One on each table.
Dirty green shade for the bar room window down
    Left.
1 saloon picture on rear wall Left of door.
1 saloon picture on Left wall upstage of window.
2 sloe-gin fizzes on tray offstage Right (lemonade).
2 gin-rickeys on tray offstage Right (lime and water).
1 highball offstage Right for SALESMAN.
Sweet Caporel box with cigarettes on table up Left
    for BELLE.
Roll of paper money for RICHARD.
60 cents in change for BARTENDER.
Several paper bills for BELLE.
Towel for BARTENDER.

## SCENE II

Newspaper (doubles from Act One) up Left end of
    table.
Sewing basket on down stage Right end of oval table.
    Spectacles, gold frame, for MRS. MILLER.
    Embroidery hoops with a piece of embroidery,
        needles and thread.

Novel of 1906 on upper Right end of oval table for
  LILY.
Practical piano off up Left.
Sheet music on piano off up Left:
  "Dearie."
  "Waiting At The Church."
  "Just Can't Make My Eyes Behave."
Pad of medium-sized paper on desk.
Pencil on desk.
The two down stage armchairs that are below the
  oval table are moved away from the table far
  enough for a person to sit on the arm of each
  that is nearest the table.
The screen door is left open for the up Curtain.


## ACT THREE

### SCENE I

### Same as Act One, Scene One.

Cigar—off up Right for MILLER. (Cut cigar in half).
Letter in opened envelope. Copy actual words from
  script. Pages 99 & 100, off up Right for MILLER.
Letter folded in tiny squares off up Left for MIL-
  DRED.


### SCENE II

White flat-bottomed boat down just Left of Center
  and is upside down with the bow toward the
  Center.
A long heavy rope is attached to the bow of the boat
  and is drawn tightly into the woods.
Town Hall Clock Strike effect. Clock strikes 9 on
  cue.

Sand ground cloth.  Sand color in the Center and fades into a deep green.

## SCENE III

Same as Act One, Scene One.

Books on upstage Left end of oval table:
"Picture of Dorian Grey."
"Ballad of Reading Goal."
"Rubaiyat."
A book written by George B. Shaw.
Several other 1906 books.
Sewing basket on down stage Right end of oval table.
Spectacles for MRS. MILLER.
Embroidery hoops with a piece of embroidery.
Needles and thread.

138

SCENE DESIGN
SITTING ROOM
AH, WILDERNESS

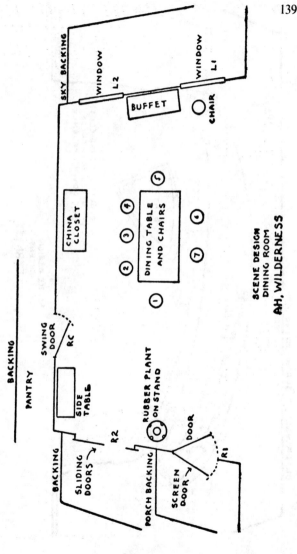

SCENE DESIGN
DINING ROOM
AH, WILDERNESS

140

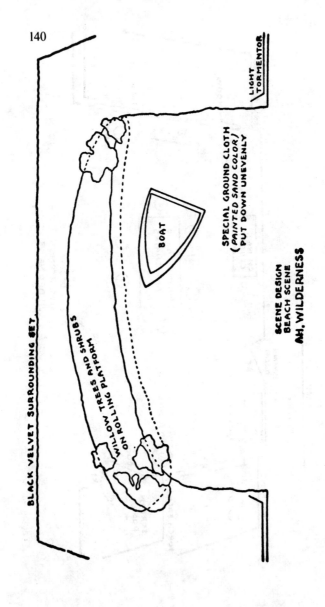

LIGHT TORMENTOR.

BLACK VELVET SURROUNDING SET.

WILLOW TREES AND SHRUBS ON ROLLING PLATFORM

BOAT

SPECIAL GROUND CLOTH
(PAINTED SAND COLOR)
PUT DOWN UNEVENLY

SCENE DESIGN
BEACH SCENE
AH, WILDERNESS

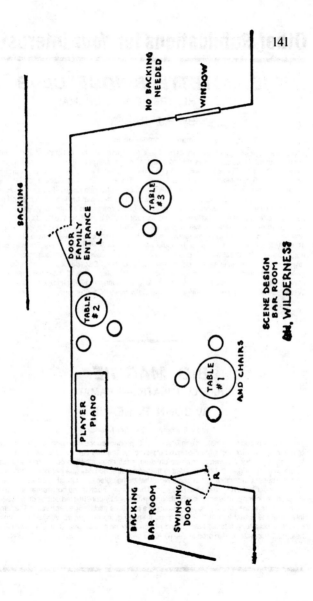

BACKING

NO BACKING NEEDED

WINDOW

TABLE #3

DOOR FAMILY ENTRANCE LC

TABLE #2

PLAYER PIANO

TABLE #1

AND CHAIRS

SCENE DESIGN
BAR ROOM
AH, WILDERNESS?

BACKING BAR ROOM

SWINGING DOOR

R

# Other Publications for Your Interest

## *THE OCTETTE BRIDGE CLUB*
### (LITTLE THEATRE—COMIC DRAMA)

### By P.J. BARRY

#### 1 man, 8 women—Interior

There are no less than *eight wonderful roles for women* in this delightful sentimental comedy about American life in the 30's and 40's. On alternate Friday evenings, eight sisters meet to play bridge, gossip and generally entertain themselves. They are a group portrait right out of Norman Rockwell America. The first act takes place in 1934; the second act, ten years later, during a Hallowe'en costume/bridge party. Each sister acts out her character, climaxing with the youngest sister's hilarious belly dance as Salome. She, whom we have perceived in the first act as being somewhat emotionally distraught, has just gotten out of a sanitarium, and has realized that she must cut the bonds that have tied her to her smothering family and strike out on her own. This wonderful look at an American family in an era far more innocent and naive than our own was quite a standout at the Actors Theatre of Louisville Humana Festival of New American Plays. The play did not succeed with Broadway's jaded critics (which these days just may be a mark in its favor); but we truly believe it is a perfect play for Everybody Else; particularly, community theatres with hordes of good actresses clamoring for roles. "One of the most charming plays to come to the stage this season . . . a delightful, funny, moving glimpse of the sort of lives we are all familiar with—our own."—NY Daily News "Counterpunch".        (#17056)

## *BIG MAGGIE*
### (LITTLE THEATRE—DRAMA)

### By JOHN B. KEANE

#### 5 men, 6 women—Exterior/Interior

We are very proud to be making available for U.S. production the most popular play by one of contemporary Ireland's most beloved playwrights. The title character is the domineering mother of four wayward, grown-up children, each determined to go his own way, as Youth will do—and each likely headed in the wrong direction. Maggie has been burdened with a bibulous, womanizing husband. Now that he has died, though, she is free to exercise some control over the lives of herself and her family, much to the consternation of her children. Wonderful character parts abound in this tightly-constructed audience-pleaser, none finer than the role of Maggie—a gem of a part for a middle-aged actress! "The feminist awareness that informs the play gives it an intriguing texture, as we watch it unfold against a colorfully detailed background of contemporary rural Ireland. It is at times like hearing Ibsen with an Irish brogue."—WWD.        (#4637)

# Other Publications for Your Interest

## *NOISES OFF*
### (LITTLE THEATRE—FARCE)

### By MICHAEL FRAYN

#### 5 men, 4 women—2 Interiors

This wonderful Broadway smash hit is "a farce about farce, taking the clichés of the genre and shaking them inventively through a series of kaleidoscopic patterns. Never missing a trick, it has as its first act a pastiche of traditional farce; as its second, a contemporary variant on the formula; as its third, an elaborate undermining of it. The play opens with a touring company dress-rehearsing 'Nothing On', a conventional farce. Mixing mockery and homage, Frayn heaps into this play-within-a-play a hilarious melee of stock characters and situations. Caricatures—cheery char, outraged wife and squeaky blonde—stampede in and out of doors. Voices rise and trousers fall . . . a farce that makes you think as well as laugh."—London Times Literary Supplement. ". . . as side-splitting a farce as I have seen. Ever? *Ever.*"—John Simon, NY Magazine. "The term 'hilarious' must have been coined in the expectation that something on the order of this farce-within-a-farce would eventually come along to justify it."—N.Y. Daily News. "Pure fun."—N.Y. Post. "A joyous and loving reminder that the theatre really does go on, even when the show falls apart."—N.Y. Times.                                                        (#16052)

## *THE REAL THING*
### (ADVANCED GROUPS—COMEDY)

### By TOM STOPPARD

#### 4 men, 3 women—Various settings

The effervescent Mr. Stoppard has never been more intellectually—and *emotionally*—engaging than in this "backstage" comedy about a famous playwright named Henry Boot whose second wife, played on Broadway to great acclaim by Glenn Close (who won the Tony Award), is trying to merge "worthy causes" (generally a euphemism for left-wing politics) with her art as an actress. She has met a "political prisoner" named Brodie who has been jailed for radical thuggery, and who has written an inept play about how property is theft, about how the State stifles the Rights of The Individual, etc., etc., etc. Henry's wife wants him to make the play work theatrically, which he does after much soul-searching. Eventually, though, he is able to convince his wife that Brodie is emphatically *not* a victim of political repression. He is, in fact, a *thug*. Famed British actor Jeremy Irons triumphed in the Broadway production (Tony Award), which was directed to perfection by none other than Mike Nichols (Tony Award). "So densely and entertainingly packed with wit, ideas and feelings that one visit just won't do . . . Tom Stoppard's most moving play and the most bracing play anyone has written about love and marriage in years."—N.Y. Times. "Shimmering, dazzling theatre, a play of uncommon wit and intelligence which not only thoroughly delights but challenges and illuminates our lives."—WCBS-TV. 1984 Tony Award-Best Play.                                                        (#941)

# Other Publications for Your Interest

## *TALKING WITH...*
### (LITTLE THEATRE)
### By JANE MARTIN

#### 11 women—Bare stage

Here, at last, is the collection of eleven extraordinary monologues for eleven actresses which had them on their feet cheering at the famed Actors Theatre of Louisville—audiences, critics and, yes, even jaded theatre professionals. The mysteriously pseudonymous Jane Martin is truly a "find", a new writer with a wonderfully idiosyncratic style, whose characters alternately amuse, move and frighten us always, however, speaking to us from the depths of their souls. The characters include a baton twirler who has found God through twirling; a fundamentalist snake handler, an ex-rodeo rider crowded out of the life she has cherished by men in 3-piece suits who want her to dress up "like Minnie damn Mouse in a tutu"; an actress willing to go to any length to get a job; and an old woman who claims she once saw a man with "cerebral walrus" walk into a McDonald's and be healed by a Big Mac. "Eleven female monologues, of which half a dozen verge on brilliance."—London Guardian. "Whoever (Jane Martin) is, she's a writer with an original imagination."—Village Voice. "With Jane Martin, the monologue has taken on a new poetic form, intensive in its method and revelatory in its impact."—Philadelphia Inquirer. "A dramatist with an original voice . . . (these are) tales about enthusiasms that become obsessions, eccentric confessionals that levitate with religious symbolism and gladsome humor."—N.Y. Times. *Talking With* . . . is the 1982 winner of the American Theatre Critics Association Award for Best Regional Play.                    (#22009)

## *HAROLD AND MAUDE*
### (ADVANCED GROUPS—COMEDY)
### By COLIN HIGGINS

#### 9 men, 8 women—Various settings

Yes: *the Harold and Maude!* This is a stage adaptation of the wonderful movie about the suicidal 19 year-old boy who finally learns how to truly *live* when he meets up with that delightfully whacky octogenarian, Maude. Harold is the proverbial Poor Little Rich Kid. His alienation has caused him to attempt suicide several times, though these attempts are more cries for attention than actual attempts. His peculiar attachment to Maude, whom he meets at a funeral (a mutual passion), is what saves him—and what captivates us. This new stage version, a hit in France directed by the internationally-renowned Jean-Louis Barrault, will certainly delight both afficionados of the film and new-comers to the story. "Offbeat upbeat comedy."—Christian Science Monitor.                    (#10032)